How You Can Have Joy

by
Vicki Jamison-Peterson

FROM THE DESK OF
PAULETTE L. BROGDEN

Vicki Jamison-Peterson Ministries
P.O. Box 700030 • Tulsa, OK 74170

Revised Edition 1985
Copyright © 1976
ISBN 0-88144-054-X
Vicki Jamison-Peterson
All Rights Reserved

Printed in U.S.
Permission granted for use of quotations from
Amplified Bible, Old Testament
                       Zondervan Publishing House
Amplified Bible, New Testament
                          The Lockman Foundation

Cover Photograph: Jeanne Kornhaber

CONTENTS

1. Joy Is Not a Feeling 9
2. Fellowship with the Father 13
3. ". . . Joy Comes in the Morning" 19
4. Joy in the Power of His Name 33
5. Heavenly Joy 47
6. The Joy of Giving 61
7. The Joy of Receiving 71
8. The Joy of Larry Lea 85
9. A Legacy of Joy 95
10. Sowing in Tears . . . Reaping in Joy 107
11. Why Do We Lose Our Joy? 119

INTRODUCTION

There is a difference between joy and happiness. To the casual observer it is slight. However, to the person who has experienced both there is an obvious difference. True joy is not dependent upon circumstances but overcomes them.

As Jesus talked with His disciples prior to Calvary, He said to them, "I will see you again and your hearts will rejoice and no one can take from you your joy" (John 16:22, *Amplified Bible*). Therefore, it is something which is available to each one of us and to which we are entitled. However, all too often it is elusive in the life of the believer. The purpose of this book is to share with the reader some of the experiences the Lord has given me and some of the lessons He has taught me about this extraordinary quality of joy and how every child of God can appropriate it and experience it in his own life.

The possibility of such joy awakens within us as we come to an understanding of what it is and what our part should be in allowing joy to burst forth from our inner being. As you learn to release the joy of the Lord, it will change your life — with God as well as with others. New horizons will open to you as you discover that there is a potential for joy in every situation of life.

1
Joy Is Not a Feeling

Joy is not a feeling, it is a fact. There is a song that says, "Joy is the flag flown high from the castle of my heart, for the King is in residence there."

There is one joy, but there are two manifestations of that joy. One is an impartation of the Holy Spirit in a moment of crisis when we are incapable of tranquil emotions, and the Comforter imparts to us that which is needed.

This was the joy that I experienced following the loss of a loved one. This is the joy that Elizabeth van Maanen experienced when her husband went to be with Jesus (see Chapter 3). Neither of us knew how to release the joy within us for we were both young in our walk with the Lord. But the Holy Spirit at such times comes to walk alongside us as well as

How You Can Have Joy

in us. Jesus said in John 14:16,17, "And I will ask the Father, and He will give you another Comforter that He may remain with you forever, The Spirit of Truth, Whom the world cannot receive because it does not see Him, nor know and recognize Him. But you know and recognize Him, for He lives with you and will be in you" *(Amplified Bible)*.

One of the offices of the Holy Spirit is the office of Comforter. And that Comforter imparts to us whatever we happen to need for the moment. This is in direct relationship to the prayer Jesus prayed for us in John 17:13: "And now I am coming to You. I say these things while I am still in the world, so that My joy may be made full and complete and perfect in them — that they may experience My delight fulfilled in them, that My enjoyment may be perfected in their souls, that they have My gladness within them filling their hearts" *(Amplified Bible)*.

The other manifestation of joy is the joy that is the fruit of the Spirit, which we ourselves are responsible for developing through the study of God's Word. This joy is included in the nine fruits of the Spirit mentioned in Galatians 5:22,23. It is interesting to note that joy is the second fruit

Joy Is Not a Feeling

of the Spirit mentioned in this passage of scripture. It immediately follows love. The other fruits of the Spirit are: peace, patience, kindness, goodness, faithfulness, gentleness and self-control.

These fruits of the Spirit have to grow in each one of us. And the joy that is a fruit of the Spirit is something that has grown in my life. I do not awaken every morning feeling joyful. I do not walk through my days with joy always. Very frankly, I have to make a conscious effort to release the joy of the Lord, just as I do to continually walk in love. I make these choices daily. They grow with knowledge of the Word of God and the experiences of victory when that knowledge has been acted upon. And I am finding they can be just as automatic as driving my car. I do not stop and think, that is a stop sign. But my reflexes remind me that a stop sign is there; and many times, unaware of what I am doing, I have driven my car throughout the city performing various duties as a driver, although I was not consciously aware of any of them. Thus it is in the dimension of joy as a fruit of the Spirit.

The paths of my life have prepared me for greater joy than ever before. And though joy

How You Can Have Joy

may not always be evident, it is nonetheless there and can be released whenever I recount the glorious deeds of God and recite His Word. "You meet and spare him who joyfully works righteousness — uprightness and justice — [earnestly] remembering You in Your ways" (Isaiah 64:5, *Amplified Bible*).

As we have fellowship with the Father and tell others about His wonderful delivering power, we can then be borne aloft on wings of joy.

2
Fellowship with the Father

Ultimate joy comes from a personal relationship with our Heavenly Father. ". . . In thy presence is fullness of joy . . ." (Psalm 16:11). The other opportunities to develop our joy have to begin in this vital relationship with God.

It was in 1966 when I began to know God personally through His Word that I experienced the fullness of joy in His presence. Each morning I would arise and eagerly grab my Bible, knowing it was a personal love message from God to me for that day. As I would walk into my den and look out the window, I would say in my heart, "I love you, Father. Lead me in your Word to that which you would speak to my heart today." And through this an intimate relationship developed so that when I needed

How You Can Have Joy

guidance, the Lord would direct me in His Word to a particular book, chapter and verse, and the communication became very personal.

As I reflect on this experience I can see now that it was the first time in my life I had experienced the fullness of joy. And it came about as I studied and meditated on the Word of God.

Psalm 16 was especially meaningful to me as I took it verse by verse, praying the Word of God back to the Father. For the Bible says in Isaiah 55:11, "So shall My word be that goes forth out of My mouth; it shall not return to Me void — without producing any effect, useless — but it shall accomplish that which I please and purpose, and it shall prosper in the thing for which I sent it" *(Amplified Bible)*.

Below is Psalm 16 from the *Amplified Bible*. As you thoughtfully read aloud each verse, you will see how dynamic it can be to quote the Word of God in prayer, remembering that God and His Word are one.

Keep and protect me, O God, for in You I have found refuge, and in You do I put my trust and hide myself.
I say to the Lord, You are my Lord; I have no good beside or beyond You.

Fellowship with the Father

As for the godly (the saints) who are in the land, they are excellent, the noble, and the glorious, in whom is all my delight.

Their sorrows shall be multiplied who choose another god; their drink offerings of blood will I not offer or take their names upon my lips.

The Lord is my chosen and assigned portion, my cup; You hold and maintain my lot.

The lines are fallen for me in pleasant places; yes, I have a good heritage.

I will bless the Lord Who has given me counsel; yes, my heart instructs me in the night seasons.

I have set the Lord continually before me; because he is at my right hand, I shall not be moved.

Therefore my heart is glad, and my glory (my inner self) rejoices; my body too shall rest and confidently dwell in safety.

For You will not abandon me to Sheol (the place of the dead), neither will You suffer Your holy one to see corruption.

You will show me the path of life; in Your presence is fullness of joy, at Your right hand there are pleasures for evermore.

How You Can Have Joy

The joy of fellowship with the Father comes as we know Him, as we read His Word, and as we speak that Word back to Him.

Fellowship with the Father is not a posture, it is not a place. But it can and should be continual. It is these moments of fellowship when we are quiet in our spirit that He often speaks to us. It can also be a preparation and an attitude without words even being spoken — a time of merely being still and knowing that He is. Just as we need this vital relationship with the ones we love, so it is even more important that we have this time apart, daily experiencing the fullness of joy through the presence of a loving Father.

The word "prayer" has frightened many people because it speaks of a religious posture or practice that has been boring or repetitious, one that has been a burdensome chore. Others look upon prayer as fearfully bowing before an awesome Presence to ask for something. However, this is not fellowshiping. Fellowshiping with the Father is merely talking with God. This can be done while driving an automobile, walking through a department store, or raking leaves. When we have fellowship with the Father we have a

Fellowship with the Father

continual awareness of His presence. We have a direct line to the throne room of God.

God's presence can become as the beautiful fragrance of perfume. You can put it on when you begin your day, and its aroma stays with you and lingers everywhere you go. Although many times you may become unaware of it, others sense its fragrance. It is there. It remains.

Fellowshipping with the Father is being unafraid; it is knowing He has forgiven your sins and loves you and wants you to come and talk to Him about everything. He enjoys having you walk into His presence and just say, "I love you, Father," instead of coming in fear or coming only when you have a request.

On our level of understanding, fellowshipping with God is the same as meeting a very dear friend over a cup of coffee and congenially talking. It is that easy. The dividend is an intimate relationship and the glow of joy.

3
". . . Joy Comes in the Morning"

On a Friday morning a number of years ago my telephone rang. When I answered it, I learned that a very dear friend of mine, named Myrtle, had gone to be with Jesus. Myrtle was one of my dearest friends, although early in our friendship I didn't fully understand or appreciate her. She was a woman who was both scholarly and shy, perfectly willing to stay in the background. As the years passed I began to see the true beauty of this woman who was always willing to be my friend and to help me with whatever I might need.

As I hung up the phone that day, my mind was flooded with memories of Myrtle. I recalled how, when she came to visit, one

How You Can Have Joy

of her greatest pleasures was to go to a nice restaurant for lunch followed by an afternoon of shopping. I thought about the many valuable lessons Myrtle had taught me about the elderly. Her last years were years of sickness. She endured much pain, and her activities were greatly restricted so that she could no longer enjoy the things she once had enjoyed. Her final years were lived in semi-confinement. As greatly as I loved Myrtle, I found myself experiencing petty annoyance at seeing medicine bottles scattered around on all the cabinets and tiny rubber bands wrapped around everything. Having rarely been around elderly people, I didn't understand their ways or habits, but as I came to understand and love Myrtle, my petty annoyance melted away. Now, hearing of her death, I was relieved to know she had been released from the pain she had endured during the last several years. My feelings on this day were those of relief for her but of great sorrow and loss for myself.

When I arrived in Angleton to make the funeral arrangements and dispose of her belongings, I suddenly felt overwhelmed. I was overcome with all the responsibilities of handling the affairs of one who has just died.

". . . Joy Comes in the Morning"

As I went through her clothing and personal possessions I almost felt as if I were an intruder. Her cherished treasures were the many books she had acquired throughout her lifetime, for she loved to read. She was a continuous student until the time of her death.

I spent the entire day sorting and packing things, answering telephone calls from sympathetic friends and loved ones, and greeting the many who came to call and offer their condolences. Food was brought in by neighbors, family and friends. This custom, still prevalent in the South, is a warm gesture of love from those who do not know what to do in a time of bereavement, when a vacuum has been left by the one who has departed. Much warmth and love can be expressed in a bowl of potato salad.

That night before going to bed I looked at the bookshelf which Myrtle's husband had built for her many years before. Since I usually read before going to sleep, I wanted to select a book. There were only a few books left that hadn't been packed yet, and I was attracted to a small booklet with a bright gold cover entitled <u>Intra Muros</u> by Rebecca Ruter Springer. I wondered what "Intra Muros" meant. My curiosity aroused, I opened the

How You Can Have Joy

cover to read the explanation, "My Dream of Heaven." As I eagerly began to devour the book, it was as if I had been transported out of the dimension of reality into another sphere. In the pages of this book I saw the streets of glory and the loved ones who had departed as they were reunited with Rebecca Springer, the book's author.

As I shared the awesomeness of the river of life and the joyous family reunions, I was elevated to a dimension of joy such as I had never before experienced. I was reminded of the words of the Psalmist, ". . . Weeping may endure for a night, but joy comes in the morning" (Psalm 30:5, *Amplified Bible*). My grief literally dissolved. My desire to try to comprehend life faded into nothingness. My spirit was so one with the Father and so one with His Son, Jesus, that I truly knew Myrtle was alive and that for the first time she was free. And she knew joy, real joy. I could hardly sleep that night for the exhilaration of this discovery. I understood what the apostle Paul meant when he wrote, ". . . Death is swallowed up in victory . . . But thanks be to God, which giveth us the victory through our Lord Jesus Christ" (I Cor. 15:54,57).

The next afternoon as I entered the little Methodist church where the organ was play-

". . . Joy Comes in the Morning"

ing softly and the casket was surrounded by lovely flowers, this supernatural joy that had been imparted to me the night before by the Holy Spirit began to burst forth within me. Rather than feeling mournful, I felt like laughing. I felt like standing before the weeping mourners and announcing, "Myrtle isn't here. She is with Jesus. She is truly free!"

It was as though I had been enclosed in a large bubble and nothing from the outside could penetrate to hurt or grieve me. I was protected, loved and cared for, and I was resting in the greatest peace and tranquility I had ever known in what should have been an hour of great sorrow and heaviness of heart. When feelings of guilt would begin to nag at me for my lack of sorrow, they would instantly disappear to be replaced by the broad embrace of joy.

This experience was one of many lessons the Lord was to teach me about the joy of the Lord. "Thou wilt shew me the path of life: in thy presence is fullness of joy; at thy right hand there are pleasures for evermore" (Psa. 16:11). The Lord was showing me the joy of the path of life, that in His presence, the presence of the living God, there is fullness of joy. Myrtle was experiencing this in a dimension I have not yet known. But I can know His presence as I fellowship with the Father, as I daily walk with Him and talk with Him.

This unaccountable joy in the midst of sorrow and loss was also experienced by Elizabeth Van Maanen, whom I first met several years ago when I was active in Lay Witness Missions. This organization in Methodist churches has been mightily used of the Lord, and the people who work it are everyday laymen and laywomen who have had a born-again experience and many of whom have had a deeper spiritual commitment.

Those of us who ministered together on lay witness teams became very close friends as we worked together in a weekend of ministry. We would meet to pray for the services, for the people and for one another, lifting each other up to the Lord.

It was during one of these weekends that I met the effervescent Elizabeth van Maanen. When a friend introduced Elizabeth to me she said, "You must meet Elizabeth van Maanen — she has a ministry of joy." To look at her radiant, smiling face and see the joy portrayed there made everyone a believer that truly she did have a ministry of joy.

". . . Joy Comes in the Morning"

A number of years later Elizabeth was a guest on my show, "It's a New Day," a daily CBN television program which I did for two seasons. Then I learned the story of how she walked into this life of constant joy, which has flowed over into many lives since then, causing them to experience this same joy. She also shared with me and with our viewers the story of the loss of her husband, whom she deeply loved, and the impartation of joy from the Holy Spirit that came to her at that time.

Elizabeth is a resident of Dallas, Texas, where her husband, Herman, was senior vice-president of First National Bank. An active member of the Episcopal church and a member of the order of St. Luke, Elizabeth works with fellow Episcopalians to help them experience the assurance of salvation and to know the reality of Jesus Christ, both as Saviour and as Healer, and to lead them into the deeper experience of the baptism in the Holy Spirit. I have asked her to tell her story here.

Elizabeth van Maanen's Testimony

As far back as I can remember, Jesus was always very real to me. I can recall many instances while I was growing up when I

How You Can Have Joy

would pray in faith believing and the Lord would answer my prayers and do wonderful things for me. But it was in 1965 that I really made Jesus the Lord of my life.

I had gone to Nacogdoches, Texas, with some friends to attend a special three-day meeting conducted by Dr. William S. Reed. Most of the sessions were held in one of the meeting rooms of a hotel, but some were conducted in a Methodist church directly across the street from the hotel. It was in a meeting in this little Methodist church that Jesus became more real to me than He ever had before.

During the service I felt a tremendous weight of sin upon me and was aware of the need for repentance and cleansing within my heart. It was not as if I had committed any horrible sins, but I experienced a feeling of unworthiness and uncleanness much the same as the prophet Isaiah must have felt when he cried, "Woe is me! for I am undone; because I am a man of unclean lips, and I dwell in the midst of a people of unclean lips: for mine eyes have seen the King, the Lord of hosts" (Isaiah 6:5).

When the invitation was given for any who desired prayer to come forward, I

". . . Joy Comes in the Morning"

quickly made my way to the altar. As hands were laid on me and the prayer of faith was prayed, I suddenly felt God's peace. The burden of sin lifted and I was set free. I returned to my seat with a lighter heart and a joyful spirit. I had experienced John's baptism of repentance. Later that night Jesus was to baptize me in the Holy Spirit!

After the service my friends and I returned to the hotel. Several had gathered to pray and a number were being filled with the Holy Spirit with the evidence of speaking in other tongues. I was more an interested spectator than an active participant, but I was hungry for more of God. And Jesus said, "Blessed are they which do hunger and thirst after righteousness: for they shall be filled" (Matt. 5:6).

While I was watching someone who was speaking in other tongues, a precious woman minister noticed me and felt impressed of the Spirit to say to her husband, "She needs her tongue loosed," at which he laid hands on me and immediately my tongue was used as an instrument of praise to God in His beautiful heavenly language. God had filled me with the Holy Spirit.

This thrilling experience was but the opening door into greater heights of spiritual blessing. I was happier than I had ever been in my life, and for the first time I was truly at peace.

Some time later I went with a friend to Fort Worth where we attended a morning Bible teaching session. (This, too, was in a Methodist church. So many wonderful things have happened to me at Methodist altars!) At the close of the meeting prayer was offered for the sick. I was sitting toward the back and didn't really have any specific need for prayer. As I watched the people being prayed for, everyone seemed very serious and intense and I wondered: Why don't they pray for joy? Finally I did go forward for prayer and when the woman who was going to pray for me laid hands on my head, she suddenly broke out in a holy laughter. Then she said, "Do you want to know what the Lord is saying to you?"

"Yes," I answered.

"The Lord is saying, 'I have saved you from folly, and I have filled you with joy. I want you to let it spill out on everyone else.' "

From that time forward I have been filled with a supernatural joy, and it is easy to let it spill out on everyone else. It is a joy that comes from the Holy Spirit. Before this

". . . Joy Comes in the Morning"

experience I had always been quite sober-minded and serious. A conscientious student, I had been named valedictorian of my high school and was Phi Beta Kappa at the University of Texas. I had always wanted to please everyone and do what was right. Now, however, the only one I really want to please is the Lord. And it pleases Him for me to be filled with His joy and to be free from the cares of this world. I was set free from my old temperament to minister joy to others, and to help those who are sorrowing to experience this same joy that I have found. ". . . That we may be able to comfort them . . . by the comfort wherewith we ourselves are comforted of God" (II Cor. 1:4).

The following year after God imparted to me His heavenly joy, I was to need it in a totally unexpected way.

For thirty years my husband Herman and I had a deep and lasting love affair. We were two people with totally different personalities which complemented each other, and our home was one of happiness and harmony. Herman and I were good friends.

Nine years prior to his death Herman had a severe heart attack and it appeared that I might lose him then. At the time I made a

How You Can Have Joy

decision that he belonged to the Lord and I committed him to God. But He gave him back to me. In the long months of convalescence that were to follow, we learned many rich and valuable spiritual lessons. It was a time which drew us closer to each other and to the Lord.

My husband recovered completely from his heart attack, and our next nine years together were among the happiest of our marriage. Then he began having further problems with his heart. He was hospitalized three times, and on his third trip to the hospital the doctor's reports were not encouraging.

At seven o'clock on the morning of May 24, 1966, the special nurse who was attending my husband called me and told me that he had taken a turn for the worse, and that I should come to the hospital right away. I got in my car and started driving toward the hospital. As I drove along Turtle Creek Boulevard, I was praying in the Spirit when suddenly an unsurpassed peace came over me and a feeling of unexplainable joy welled up within me. I was literally surprised by joy. It was as if the heavens had opened and I could hear the singing of the heavenly host praising God. In that instant I knew my husband had just gone to be with Jesus—that

". . . Joy Comes in the Morning"

he had at that moment been ushered into His presence by that glorious heavenly host.

When I reached the hospital I took the elevator to the ninth floor. Getting off the elevator, I was greeted by the doctor who gently said, "Herman has just gone."

"I know," I said, "It's all right. Would you mind if I just shed a few tears?" and I put my head on his shoulder. After a few moments my tears were gone, and since that time I have never known any grief.

At the funeral service on the following Thursday, my feelings were not those of grief and sorrow but of compassion for the people who were there. For everyone looked very sad and forlorn. Yet in my heart there was no sadness. I wished that I could comfort the people the way I was being comforted.

Later the Lord was to direct me to the passage in Isaiah: "Fear not; for thou shalt not be ashamed . . . for thou . . . shalt not remember the reproach of thy widowhood any more. For thy Maker is thine husband; the Lord of hosts is his name . . ." (Isaiah 54:4, 5). This entire 54th chapter has been a great comfort to me in the years since Herman went to be with the Lord, for it is filled with numerous promises of God's love and concern for the widowed.

How You Can Have Joy

I have learned that death is not grim. It is the door into that wonderful land with the Lord. And even when death separates us from those whom we hold dearest in life, we can experience God's heavenly joy.

4
Joy in the Power of His Name

Since childhood I had heard stories of Satan — how evil he is and how powerful. I had the typical mental image of him as someone with horns on his head, wearing a red suit and carrying a pitchfork.

I continued to believe that Satan was all-powerful until I discovered the scripture which says that all power has been given to us in the name of Jesus. "Behold! I have given you authority and power to trample upon serpents and scorpions, and (physical and mental strength and ability) over all the power that the enemy possesses, and nothing shall in any way harm you" (Luke 10:19, *Amplified Bible*).

Many Christians needlessly accept the continual harassment from the devil, not

How You Can Have Joy

knowing that they have authority over him. However, God's Word shows that our loving Heavenly Father has a different plan for our lives. We are to be full of love and joy and victory. When these cease to be prevalent in us, it is due to the power of the enemy.

Among the many lessons that God was to teach me about joy was this: *There is a joy that comes to the believer as he exercises his authority in the all-powerful name of Jesus.*

Although I had heard of the power that resides in the name of Jesus, I had had no experience at all in using that name. My first encounter with the power of His name came when I went to a Full Gospel Business Men's convention in Los Angeles, California, some years ago. I had only recently begun to really follow the Lord at that time, and was thrilled to have this opportunity to hear great speakers and to be blessed by the teaching of God's Word. One of my best friends was a young widow, who accompanied me to the convention.

We were hardly out of the city when she became violently ill. She was sick during most of our three-day trip from Dallas to Los Angeles, suffering greatly with an intense migraine headache. We stopped frequently to

Joy in the Power of His Name

buy ice for her, and did everything we could think of to ease her pain and to make her more comfortable.

Finally we arrived in Los Angeles and checked into the Beverly Hilton Hotel where the FGBMFI convention was being held. Because she was so very ill I tried to spend as much time as possible with her, praying for her and claiming the promise in the Word that by the stripes of Jesus she was healed. But instead of growing better, she only seemed to grow worse. The pressure in her head was so great that she couldn't even bear to have a light on in the room.

Realizing I was missing most of the convention, I began to attend some of the services, leaving her alone in the room. Listening to the Word of God being taught in the services, I became aware that it was an evil spirit which was causing my friend to suffer such devastating pain, and that I had authority over this spirit. I went back to her room in anger — not at her, but at Satan for causing her to miss the blessings of the Lord, and for causing us to miss hearing about what God was doing, which we so desperately needed to hear.

When I walked into her room I said, "In the name of Jesus, I rebuke and bind your

How You Can Have Joy

power, Satan." And then, although I didn't actually see a demon or an imp with my natural eyes, with my spiritual eyes I saw an evil spirit in the room. I grabbed a book and — although I don't really recommend this as a way of dealing with Satanic powers, in my inexperience this was what I felt to do — I threw this book in the direction of the evil spirit and said, "Satan, I said in the name of Jesus get out of here and don't come back." As I demanded my rights in the name of Jesus, she was totally healed. Every bit of pain and pressure left her head. She got up, dressed, and was able to eat a meal for the first time in days.

Thus began for me the adventure of knowing the power in the name of Jesus. This was to become a springboard for me, for the Lord many times allows us minor skirmishes before we as believers come into the full battle. We were to be propelled to new heights of joy as time and again in our walk of faith we were to witness the tremendous power in Jesus' name.

One such incident involved Lee and Blackie, two people whom I had met when I first moved to Dallas. Members of a very large church, Lee and Blackie were born-again believers and were active in their church and

Joy in the Power of His Name

Sunday school. Although I didn't attend that church, Lee and Blackie and I had become friends through my parents and we saw each other quite often.

After several years of casual friendship with Lee and Blackie, our relationship began to change. Their lifestyle became radically different, for instead of being involved in church activities they became caught up in a social whirl. Wanting to feel a part of the group of social drinkers they had begun associating with, they also began to drink. They certainly didn't plan to become alcoholics, they were just going to have a good time with their friends. But they were to learn that when we open the door to Satan, he is not a gentleman. He walks in and takes over.

Our lives began to go in opposite directions as there was no common ground for fellowship between us. Jesus was Lord of my life, whereas, more and more, Lee and Blackie were making alcohol the god of their lives.

Soon they began to have fights, not only verbal conflicts but physical bouts as well. Lee would start drinking as soon as she got to her job and would drink all day. Blackie was doing the same. Too late they discovered they

How You Can Have Joy

were in the grip of alcoholism and were bound by the desire to drink.

Although I talked to Lee occasionally on the phone, my mother kept in closer touch with them. She sometimes reported to me that Blackie had again been arrested for drunken driving. Each time his attorney was able to get him out of trouble; however, even his attorney became disgusted with him and grew tired of representing him.

I shall never forget the night I decided Lee needed to go to church. I felt if she could only get to church, she would be set free and her life would again become one of tranquility. She would again be the happy, buoyant person I had known. For before becoming a victim of alcoholism she had had one of the most zestful, bubbling personalities I had ever seen.

I called Lee's house and said, "Lee, I'm coming over to take you to church." When I got there she was drunk — sloppily, disgustingly drunk. I was determined, however, that she was going to church that night, so I started dressing her. As I tried to help her into her clothes, she would fall over on the bed and would lie there, muttering incoherently. Still I refused to give up. After about an hour I had her dressed and in my

Joy in the Power of His Name

car on the way to church. As we drove along, she was a pitiful sight as she tried to put on her lipstick, repeatedly missing her mouth.

I had succeeded in getting Lee to church but not in sobering her up, and she was drunk throughout the entire service. I was extremely embarrassed, and regretted that I had tried to take her to church. My efforts had met with total failure.

Although I had been praying for Lee and Blackie, I was to learn that the time for their deliverance was not of my choosing. They had to desire to be set free.

Several years passed before I was again led to contact Lee and Blackie Baskin. It happened one evening when I was dining with a friend in a restaurant close to the Baskins' home. Lee and Blackie were on my heart as I sat in that neighborhood, remembering the good days we had had with them. As we left the restaurant I said to my friend, "Let's drive by Lee and Blackie's house." My friend was hesitant to do so at first, for we had heard of their violent fights. However, after some time, my friend reluctantly agreed to stop by the Baskins' residence, and we drove to their house.

When we arrived I said, "Let's go in and see Lee and Blackie." My friend later confided

How You Can Have Joy

to me that she tried to think of every excuse in the world not to go in. Because I was so insistent, however, she finally yielded, secretly hoping no one would be at home.

We walked up to their door and rang the doorbell. Within a matter of seconds Blackie came to the door. His jaw was wired together and he was barely able to talk, but he managed to say, "Last night I dreamed you came to see us. Come In!"

We were in the living room only a few moments when I asked about Lee. Blackie said she was in the bedroom. She was trying to hide because she had been drinking and didn't want me to know. But I sought her out. Her eyes were glazed from drunkenness, and she had tried to hide the smell of alcohol on her breath with "Jungle Gardenia" perfume.

I began to talk to Lee about God's love for her, and I led her into the living room. As we sat on the sofa and I shared with her, God's love poured forth from me. I overheard my friend asking Blackie, "Are you happy, Blackie?" Blackie replied, "I was just wondering the other night how I ever got into this mess."

As Blackie and Lee both confessed their need for help and we shared with them that

Joy in the Power of His Name

God had made a way for them to be set free, they agreed to get on their knees with us and commit their lives anew to Jesus.

As we prayed we took authority over the spirit of alcoholism. We said, "In the name of Jesus, we rebuke and bind the power of Satan over Blackie and Lee according to Matthew 18:18, and in the name of Jesus, you take your hands off their lives, Satan. They belong to Jesus. You have to go!"

As we got up from prayer Lee said, "You will never know what it meant to have you come tonight." Later I was to learn that Lee had planned to commit suicide that evening.

The story continues as we were to make an important discovery about dealing with evil spirits. For at noon the next day my telephone rang and I picked it up to hear the voice of Lee. She didn't have to tell me she was drunk; I could tell by her voice. My heart sank, and the devil whispered in my ear, "It didn't work."

I remembered having heard someone say that evil spirits are subject to us, but that many times they try to test us to see if we really know our authority in Jesus' name. I decided to act upon that knowledge and I said, "Lee, I am not talking to you. I am going to talk to that spirit which holds you." I then

How You Can Have Joy

addressed the spirit and said, "I told you to go last night, and because of the power of the name of Jesus you have to obey. For Jesus defeated you; He is greater than you and you have to leave her, never to return. As I told you last night, I bind you in the name of Jesus. Your power was broken last night. You do not frighten me a bit." I was standing on the words of Jesus in Matthew 18:18: "Whatsoever ye shall bind on earth shall be bound in heaven: and whatsoever ye shall loose on earth shall be loosed in heaven."

I then addressed my remarks to Lee and said, "Lee, pour all the liquor in the house down the sink. Wherever you have hidden it (for she had stashed it in closets, dresser drawers, every place imaginable), go get it and throw it all away. Then make yourself a pot of black coffee and drink it. You will never take another drink." As I heard myself making such a bold statement, I almost wondered at my audacity. But it was the power of the Word of God within me. I was not basing this on my own knowledge, I was basing it on Mark 11:23. I was talking to the mountain of alcoholism. And because God's Word cannot fail, I rested my case before the court of heaven. This was many years ago, and Lee has never had another drink since that day.

Joy in the Power of His Name

Blackie was another story.

Blackie continued to grow worse. Now that Lee was walking with the Lord and had been filled with the Holy Spirit, Blackie began to taunt her and call her a "Holy Roller." I asked her if that wasn't better than what he used to call her. I encouraged her to stand true to the Lord, telling her that Blackie was set free the same night she was, and we were not going to back down on our confession of faith for his deliverance.

After several weeks had gone by and Blackie was still drinking quite heavily, I went over to his house one afternoon with two friends, Jeanne Kornhaber and Jo Jones. We claimed the scripture in Acts 19:11,12: "And God wrought special miracles by the hands of Paul: So that from his body were brought unto the sick handkerchiefs or aprons, and the diseases departed from them, and the evil spirits went out of them." Because the anointing of the Holy Spirit is greater than all the power of Satan, we felt impressed of the Lord to lay hands upon his clothing and especially pray over the chair in which Blackie usually sat. Anointing a handkerchief with oil, we placed it under the cushion of the seat and said, "In the name of Jesus, every spirit that

How You Can Have Joy

comes in contact with this chair and with all this clothing cannot stay."

The unique part of this story is that Blackie did not know we had been in the home or that we had prayed especially over his chair.

One month later Blackie stood before a group of men and women at a Full Gospel Business Men's Fellowship meeting and shared his story of deliverance. As he told what had happened, a spontaneous joy began to bubble up within my soul as again I saw the way the Word of God had worked.

Blackie told how he had been on a three-day drinking spree when in the middle of the night the Lord awakened him from a deep sleep and said to him, "Blackie, get up and go into the living room and sit in your chair." He got up and went into the living room and sat in the chair.

After he had been there a few moments Satan said to him, "Get up and go to bed," and he did.

A little later the Lord spoke again saying, "Blackie, get up and go sit in that chair." He got up and went to the living room and sat in the chair.

Satan said to him, "Blackie, get up from the chair and go to bed." Again he obeyed.

Joy in the Power of His Name

A third time the Lord said, "Blackie, get up and go into the living room and sit in your chair." He did so and as he sat there in the darkness he heard the audible voice of God say to Satan, "Take your hands off of him. You have had him long enough. He belongs to me." Suddenly the room was filled with a bright light, and Blackie was completely set free. He has never had a drink again to this day.

As Blackie shared this story with the men and women present that evening, he did not know we had prayed over his chair. How marvelously God honored His Word!

Today Blackie and Lee are members of a charismatic Baptist church in Dallas, and are two of its most active members. They are continually ministering to people with similar problems of alcoholism. They are living victorious, abundant and joyful lives for Jesus.

Great joy has been ours ever since we came to the full realization that even evil spirits are subject to us in the name of Jesus.

5
Heavenly Joy

Have you ever wondered what brings joy in heaven? The words of Jesus give us the answer.

"I say unto you, that likewise joy shall be in heaven over one sinner that repenteth, more than over ninety and nine just persons, which need no repentance" (Luke 15:7). "Notwithstanding in this rejoice not, that the spirits are subject unto you; but rather rejoice, because your names are written in heaven" (Luke 10:20). Jesus made this latter statement to the seventy when they returned rejoicing that devils were subject to them in the name of Jesus, and it followed Christ's admonition, "Behold, I give unto you power to tread on serpents and scorpions, and over all the power of the enemy: and nothing shall by any means hurt you" (verse 19).

How You Can Have Joy

Jesus was telling them that if the fact that demons were subject to them was cause for rejoicing, which it should be for He had given them this authority, how much more should they rejoice that their names were written in heaven!

As I travel throughout the country ministering for the Lord, the people I meet add a dimension to our lives that is rich and often full of surprises. Many lasting friendships have been made as men and women have volunteered to chauffeur me to and from airports, services, television stations and other places of ministry. These wonderful believers who have so generously given their time have also shared their stories and testimonies with me. One which I would like to share with you has certainly brought joy to heaven.

While I was in El Paso, Texas, to do a television show on I.C.T. Cable, Channel 8, a Christian television station, I met a personable young man who drove me wherever I needed to go. Not only was this my first show in El Paso, but it was also a first for the station and for me in that we were taking the mobile television unit to a shopping center to do a live one-hour production, which is a bold and innovative idea.

Heavenly Joy

As we were riding along in the car my thoughts were on the show we were about to produce, and I wasn't especially interested in talking. However, the sparkle in our driver's eyes aroused my curiosity, and I heard myself asking him questions only to discover he was the young man I had heard of through Eddie Horn, the station manager. We shall call him "Sol," although this is not his name, because his family has not yet accepted Jesus as Messiah. But we know they will. He is about the age David was when he slew Goliath. And like David, he too is a Jew.

Sol had been interested in television work since he was 14 years old and began to work for KDBC, Channel 4, a TV station in El Paso, doing whatever needed to be done around the studio. So sharp and creative is he that within a matter of months he was not only running cameras and working as an engineer, but he was also directing television programs.

When I.C.T. Cable, Channel 8, was started in El Paso, Sol went to work there as technical director, even though he himself was not a Christian. He was directing some programs when Alex Blomerth and Pete Warren realized that problems were arising through his directing because, being an unbeliever, he didn't understand the work of the Holy Spirit. So

How You Can Have Joy

they transferred him to the position of cameraman. They also began talking to him about Jesus. He told them, however, that because of his Jewish background he could not accept Jesus as the Son of God.

Several weeks passed. One night while driving home, Pete again talked to Sol about Jesus as the Messiah. As Sol entered his home that evening thinking about what Pete had said, he prayed, "OK, God, if Jesus is your Son, show me."

At this point in his story I interrupted him and asked, "How did God show you? Did you have a vision?"

"No," he replied. "I don't know what happened. I felt a joy I had never experienced in my whole life — true joy. It just came from inside me. And I never lost it since that day. It was a joy that was unknown to me, and it made me to know then that Jesus was the Son of God; and I accepted Him into my heart that night."

As he experienced the joy of salvation, heaven too was rejoicing. Heaven was filled with joy because a new name had been recorded in the Book of Life. And there is not a happier, more joyful person alive than this Jewish young man in El Paso. The joy of the

Heavenly Joy

Lord is his strength, and it is that joy which was given him, making him aware that Jesus is his Lord and bringing Christ to dwell within his heart.

An interesting postscript to Sol's story is that he is now employed by a radio station in El Paso which is owned by a group of Jewish businessmen. Although these owners are not Christians, they discovered they could make more money by having an inspirational radio station. Programs on mind control and other material that is not Christian in content although considered inspirational were being used in this format. After Sol was made program director for this station, however, he eliminated all programming that was not Christ-honoring, thus making this station a voice in the area of continual witness for the Lord.

After Jesus told His followers that they should rejoice that their names were written down in heaven, the scriptures tell us: "In that same hour He rejoiced and gloried in the Holy Spirit and said, I thank You, Father, Lord of heaven and earth, that You have concealed these things (relating to salvation) from the wise and understanding and learned, and revealed them to babes — the childish, unskilled and untaught. Yes, Father, for such

How You Can Have Joy

was Your gracious will and choice and good pleasure" (Luke 10:21, *Amplified Bible*).

Who would ever dream that Bourbon Street in New Orleans, Louisiana, would be the city where I discovered the reality of this scripture?

I intended to go to New Orleans for three days of ministry. Three days in that wicked city would be enough. From there I was to go to Louisville, Kentucky, South Bend, Indiana — my schedule was set.

On the third night of ministry in the First Assembly of God Church in New Orleans, so beautifully had the Holy Spirit ministered that we stood in awe of the power and presence of God. There were many great miracles of healing and as I stood worshiping the Lord at the end of the service, the Spirit of the Lord spoke to me in an inward but precise voice saying, "I want you to stay and minister in New Orleans."

I said, "Lord, if you want me to stay, you will have to speak to this pastor; he will have to be the one to extend the invitation." Then I turned the service back over to the Reverend Marvin Gorman, trusting God that if indeed I was to stay, this man who knows the voice of God would in obedience speak.

Heavenly Joy

As I walked away from the podium, the pastor turned to me and said, "Vicki, I feel you must stay. Will you?"

Even though I knew that other churches were expecting me and advertising was out, while the anointing of the Holy Spirit was dominating the service it was easy to say, "Yes, I'll stay."

The next few days were unlike any I have ever spent in my life. The devil was to attack our ministry in every conceivable way. For the stakes were high and many souls were to come into the Kingdom in the following two weeks. Yet the blessings of God were outpoured upon us without measure. On several occasions we ministered healing and salvation to the city of New Orleans through the medium of live television. We moved into a large meeting hall in the Superdome so that those who were uneasy in a church would freely come.

After a week of ministry in New Orleans in which we saw several hundred saved, I felt led to challenge the faithful believers who had been with us each evening. They had been taught the Word of God, and now I felt it was time for some of them to move out and begin to put their faith into action. The Bible tells

How You Can Have Joy

us to go into the highways and byways and compel the people to come in.

That evening the theme of the entire service was John 21:15-17 where Jesus asked Peter if he loved Him. "If you do, feed my sheep," the Lord told Peter. I called for those to come forward who would go with us into the streets of the French Quarter the next evening and witness publicly for Jesus Christ. About 35 people came forward, and we had a time of rejoicing in the Lord that the next evening we would go to the French Quarter to tell people that Jesus loves them.

I had never led a group of people in such an endeavor before, and quite frankly I had some apprehensions about it as I thought about it after the service. But I knew I was committed to go, and I felt God would have me to do this. My heart was burdened as I saw the sin and darkness in the French Quarter of New Orleans. Here in this beautiful and historic city where the world-renowned Mardigras takes place each year, Satan worship is practiced and witchcraft is rampant. This is Satan's ground. Now we have to go into it.

When we arrived at the church the next night, we prayed together and asked the angels of the Lord to go before us, to encamp

Heavenly Joy

about us according to Psalm 34:7. We prayed that the anointing of the Spirit might work through us to reach the lost.

The church made one of their buses available to us, and it was packed with people singing and praising the Lord as we drove to the French Quarter. We parked by the Mississippi River, and as we began to march toward the French Quarter I asked that the group remain silent. As I look back now it seems rather humorous and yet very dynamic in the Spirit, for here were some 40 people walking down the street, two and three abreast, in total silence. We were getting ready to penetrate the enemy's territory.

After walking several blocks in silence, we met a young man carrying a Bible. We had not yet reached Bourbon Street, which by this time was "swinging" with people from all over the world who had come to lose themselves in the sin and debauchery of this den of iniquity. As we passed this young man, he smiled, recognizing some of the youth among our group, for he was a regular witness in this area. As he smiled and said, "Praise the Lord!" I knew this was our cue. I said, "OK, everybody, let's sing." We began to sing, "The joy of the Lord is my strength, the joy of the Lord is my strength, the joy of

How You Can Have Joy

the Lord is my strength, the joy of the Lord is my strength. He gives me living water and I thirst no more, He gives me living water and I thirst no more, He gives me living water and I thirst no more, the joy of the Lord is my strength."*

By now we had began to approach more people, and the impact of so many voices singing this song of joy as they walked along began to draw attention. When we reached Bourbon Street we turned to the left and arriving in front of a large restaurant and hotel I said, "Stop here," for there were several hundred people having a party on the ornate, wrought-iron balcony above us. For the first time I took the public address system and began to share the love of Jesus Christ. As I did so the team members spread out and talked to individuals about Christ. Many people accepted Christ as their Saviour.

Again I felt impressed that we should sing, and so we sang, "The joy of the Lord is my strength, the joy of the Lord is my strength, the joy of the Lord is my strength, the joy of the Lord is my strength." Then we sang, "Amazing grace, how sweet the sound, that saved a wretch like me; I once was lost

---
*Composed by Alliene Vale, Houston, Texas.

Heavenly Joy

but now am found, was blind but now I see." Suddenly the people on the balcony above us stopped their partying and began to listen.

Just then the manager of the restaurant and hotel called the police to complain that we were disturbing the peace. I later learned that the police came and told the hotel manager that we were not disturbing the peace. Although we didn't know it at the time, we actually were breaking the law by using the public address system.

Throughout the evening as we walked up and down Bourbon Street, the police would come up to us; but they never asked us to move on or bothered us in any way. We broke the law in ignorance and God protected us.

We were all learning together how to witness publicly. It was also a lesson in humility, for here we were, acting the part of the fanatic that most of us had made fun of at one time or another in our lives. I had always abhorred anyone who stood on the street corner preaching. But what joy and peace we have when we know Jesus and want only to please Him and lead souls to Him.

Each time we began to march down the street, the Lord would impress me to sing the chorus, "The Joy of the Lord Is My Strength,"

How You Can Have Joy

and this became our theme song that night. I was to see the value of that song, for everyone in the French Quarter that night was there to have a good time, to have fun, to experience joy. We didn't tell them they were going to hell, we had come to share God's love.

As we sang, others would join our group who obviously had at one time known the Lord, or who knew the Lord and had no business on Bourbon Street. They would follow us and even join in the singing. We saw some who were just curious and others who were sincerely touched by the Spirit of God. We could look into their faces and see the ones whom God was dealing with by His Spirit.

As we made our way along Bourbon Street, singing "The Joy of the Lord Is My Strength," we walked past one bar so crowded that people were waiting to get inside. Some Japanese men who were waiting to get into the bar didn't fully understand what was going on, but they were so caught up with the spirit of song that they joined in and sang along with us as we walked by.

We then came to a very dark place on Bourbon Street between two elegant and famous restaurants and bars. When we reached that point, as clearly as I have ever received direction from the Lord, I heard Him say, "I want you to stop here." As we did we began to sing, "The Battle Hymn of the Republic." Following that familiar refrain the great song of praise to God, "How Great Thou Art," began to flow from our lips. As I sang I closed my eyes and lifted my hands to worship the Father, for the power of God was very real.

People began coming out onto the balcony of one of the restaurants, and these fashionably dressed men and women paused, not to make fun, but to be moved upon by the Spirit of God such as many of them had never witnessed before. So precious was this moment that it was as if the people were not there — it was just Jesus and me.

While I was singing and praising the Lord, our team members were moving from person to person leading them in the sinner's prayer. One young man threw away over $100 worth of drugs right then and there and received Jesus as his Saviour. In the service the next night he was filled with the Holy Spirit with the evidence of speaking in other

How You Can Have Joy

tongues. He also received healing for his eyes that night and no longer had to wear glasses.

Throughout that evening on Bourbon Street, many came to know Jesus as their Saviour. That night I understood how Jesus "in that same hour . . . rejoiced and gloried in the Holy Spirit," for God the Father was using the babes, the unskilled and untaught as an army to witness for Him.

6
The Joy of Giving

"Let each one give as he has made up his own mind and purposed in his heart, not reluctantly or sorrowfully or under compulsion, for God loves (that is, He takes pleasure in, prizes above other things, and is unwilling to abandon or to do without) a cheerful (joyous, prompt-to-do-it) giver — whose heart is in his giving" (II Cor. 9:7, *Amplified Bible*).

We are all eager to hear the voice of God; we are excited about what He is going to say to us. But when we hear the voice of God telling us to give sacrificially, we often wonder if perhaps it is not our imagination — or even the voice of the devil. However, I am learning that when we are prompted to give, we'd better listen because God is not only wanting to teach us a lesson but He also wants to bless us in a new way. He is desiring to add to our

How You Can Have Joy

measure of joy. For Luke 6:38 says we have to give before it can be given to us. "Give, and (gifts) will be given you, good measure, pressed down, shaken together and running over will they pour into (the pouch formed by) the bosom (of your robe and used as a bag). For with the measure you deal out — that is, with the measure you use when you confer benefits on others — it will be measured back to you" (Luke 6:38, *Amplified Bible*).

There is a joy in our spirit as we obey the voice of God in giving.

It is amusing to look back at some of my own experiences during the last few years, remembering the trauma I have felt when God spoke to me about giving sacrificially. But as I have obeyed the voice of God, a hilarity has come as a result of seeing how God has used this giving not only to bless the lives of other individuals, but to bless me as well. New frontiers, spiritual as well as material, have opened for me as I've dared to obey God.

My first experience in the area of giving with abandon was in Little Rock, Arkansas, during the first year of my ministry. Always before going to any city for a meeting we agreed in faith together that a certain amount

The Joy of Giving

of money would be provided to meet our needs. For we have been taught to act upon the Word of God, to agree in faith according to Matthew 18:19. We have learned that this is what we must do for our financial needs to be met.

At this particular time I didn't have very many invitations to minister, and I needed over $1,000 to cover our expenses for this meeting. On the first night a banquet had been scheduled, and those who invited us suggested that no offering should be received at this banquet, to which we agreed. As this was a three-day meeting, there were still two services in which the needed $1,000 could come in.

As I walked into the building the next night, I saw Russell Taff, a young man whom I had asked to come and lead the singing for us. While discussing with him the music for the evening, I heard the voice of the Spirit telling me to give him the offering that we were to receive that evening in order that he could make a record album. Russell has a beautiful voice, and at this time he was working with Hettie Lou Brooks at Brookhill Ranch (the "Holy Barn") in Hot Springs, Arkansas, in ministering to the youth.

How You Can Have Joy

Immediately I began to argue that (1) this couldn't be the Lord because thus far I had received no money and I was paying all of my own expenses; and (2) that would mean there would be only one more service in which to receive an offering, and my needs were so great it would be almost impossible for the needed amount of money to come in in one evening. For at that time my faith wasn't sufficient to believe God for $1,000 in a single service. But again I heard the voice of the Lord telling me, "Give Russell the offering tonight for an album."

Again I reasoned with the Lord, "It's not possible. I must have this money for expenses I have right now."

Later during the service while Russell was leading the singing I again felt this same prompting of the Holy Spirit. But still I was unwilling to obey because I was looking at the practical side of the ministry.

When the time came to receive the evening offering, I asked Russell to tell the people that this was their opportunity to share in our ministry. While the ushers were receiving the offering, the Lord strongly moved upon my heart that I *must* obey Him.

I stepped to the podium, placed my arm around Russell and said, "All of you are

The Joy of Giving

familiar with the beauty of this voice and with this young man's dedication to the Lord. God wants him to have a record album, and we are going to give him this offering, which we have just received to be used for that purpose. Anyone who would like to have a part in helping Russell with this album and would like to add to this, please come forward and place your money on this open Bible." While Russell sang, "Amazing Grace," the people joyfully came forward and placed their offerings on the Bible, giving a total amount above that which had already been received, so eager were they to help Russell with this album.

The remainder of the service was gloriously blessed of the Lord, and the minute the service was over I experienced the joy of the Lord much as the 120 did on the Day of Pentecost when all who were in Jerusalem thought the believers were drunk. For I experienced a dimension of the Holy Spirit that was new to me and that was a literal drunkenness in the Holy Spirit with the joy of the Lord.

I understand now why the Lord allowed this to happen to me. For fear would try to seize my heart and rob me of the great victory of obeying God. The Holy Spirit, knowing

How You Can Have Joy

all things, immersed me in a joyful hilarity and laughter.

We went to a restaurant for a snack following the service, and this joyful laughter continued. I was even disturbing the tables around us, which is uncharacteristic of me, but I couldn't quit laughing for the joy was that intense. Jeanne Kornhaber, our office manager, and Sharon Bell-Stromley, my accompanist, were also caught up in this hilarity, so there were now three of us with what some would consider questionable behavior.

The next morning as I awoke I thought, "Oh, Lord, what have I done? I have given everything away. We have hotel bills to pay as well as traveling expenses."

Then God's peace flooded my heart and He said, "Don't worry about it. My Word will work." My understanding of the way His Word would work was that the money would come in the offering that evening. This was not to be God's way, however. As a matter of fact, the offering was rather small that night.

As we drove back to Dallas at the conclusion of this meeting my mind was a battleground between fear and faith — with fear seeming to come out ahead. I wondered: Was I foolish to give everything away?

The Joy of Giving

One week later I walked to the mailbox and took from it a letter from someone who had been in the service in Little Rock the night we gave the offering to Russell. The letter said, ". . . The Lord spoke to me and told me to send this check to you . . ." The check was for the full amount of both offerings we had received that night. Had I not obeyed the Lord, our offering would have met only half of the budget. But by obeying the voice of God and giving the people an opportunity to give to Russell, the Lord combined both amounts and met the entire need.*

There is a joyfulness in giving. God loves a "cheerful, joyous, prompt-to-do-it giver whose heart is in his giving." One of the greatest joys I've had in serving God is the joy of giving to others, not only of money but also of time, of love, and of every area of my life. As we give we receive because His Word teaches this spiritual principle, and it has to operate as our trust is in God and in His Word.

I was to minister in Little Rock again, and it was here that through the dedicated lives

---

*In 1984 it was my greatest joy to witness Russell Taff win a Grammy as the best gospel vocalist in America. The seed I had sown in the early '70's brought an abundant harvest through this great singer. He reaches thousands now — my seed lives forever planted in joy.

How You Can Have Joy

of Cecil Pumphrey and his beautiful wife the Lord would teach me another important lesson about giving.

I was always aware of the Pumphreys' presence in the services because of their happy, smiling faces, and the love which emanated from them. My knowledge of their background was sketchy. I had been told that Cecil had pastored a Baptist Church. But when he received the fullness of the Holy Spirit, he was no longer welcome in his church. Cecil was always a very joyful Christian, and even though he no longer had a church to pastor, he was busy ministering to others. He was quick to tell everyone what God was doing in his life.

One morning at the end of a teaching session, I gave the people an opportunity to share in the expenses of the meeting. Very little was said about the offering, but I remember praying that morning, "Father, I ask you to repay a hundredfold everyone who gives in this offering." To my knowledge I had never prayed that prayer before.

While the ushers were receiving the offering, my attention was drawn to Cecil, and the Lord gently whispered, "I want you to receive an offering for Cecil."

The Joy of Giving

I stood and said, "We all know and love Cecil, and I feel impressed in my spirit that today we are to share with Cecil and his wife. So if you have something which God has placed on your heart to give to them, as the service concludes come forward and place it on the podium."

I was later to learn why God moved on me in this manner. For a principle of giving had been activated, and God would move heaven and earth if necessary to honor the faith and obedience of one of His children.

That morning as I received the offering, Cecil had turned to his wife and said, "What do we have to give?"

"We have only $2, and we need that to pay for our parking tonight," she answered. They were counselors for a Billy Graham film which was showing in downtown Little Rock.

Cecil said, "Let's give it in the offering." He had learned the principles of giving and was unafraid to obey God. He knew that as he obeyed, the doors of heaven would swing open to pour out blessings in abundance.

They had barely placed their last $2 in the offering plate when the Spirit of the Lord spoke to me, and I stood and shared my burden with the people that morning, although I really did not know Cecil or his

How You Can Have Joy

wife and did not know they had a need. But when they gave everything they had, even though it was only $2, God moved in their behalf and the offering that came in amounted to $210. Within 15 minutes God had given back to them a hundredfold.

Together we experienced the joy of the Lord as Cecil and his wife shared with me what had happened. I have known of larger gifts, but never of larger hearts. For what could be greater than giving your last $2 in an act of obedience, and seeing the hand of a loving Father move in your behalf?

7
The Joy of Receiving

Numerous books have been written and lengthy sermons have been preached on the joy of giving. And this is scriptural. Yet an equally important but often overlooked joy is the joy of receiving. Most people are reluctant to admit that it is fun to receive, thinking it reflects selfishness. Children, however, have no such inhibitions and don't try to conceal their eagerness as they count the days until Christmas in anticipation of the gifts they will receive. God wants His children to be blessed not only in the act of giving but also in the experience of receiving. "Every good gift and every perfect gift is from above, and cometh down from the Father . . ." (James 1:17).

There is an art to receiving in a manner that will bring joy to the giver as well as to

How You Can Have Joy

the receiver. It was only in recent years that I began to recognize the value of this art.

All my life I've had a deep appreciation for things of beauty. It has always brought me a special thrill to receive a cherished object. Several years ago I realized, however, that I was not expressing outwardly the inner excitement I felt when someone gave me a lovely present. Knowing how much pleasure it gave me when a friend was genuinely delighted by a gift I had given, I began to make a conscious effort to show my true feelings when I received a gift. Soon my lips were able to express the joy I felt in my heart. And I saw that I could enhance the giver's joy by letting my delight burst forth spontaneously from the depths of my being.

By allowing this pleasure that is yours as a recipient to flow freely from you into the life of the one who has given, you will both be blessed. Thus the joy of giving intermingles with the joy of receiving.

One of my early lessons in the art of receiving will be remembered the rest of my life as a turning point in my ministry. For a year and a half I had been teaching people that God would supply all of their needs according to His riches in glory by Christ Jesus, if they would act upon certain

The Joy of Receiving

principles of faith, totally trusting God that He would honor their faith and abundantly supply their daily needs. Yet I now found myself facing a tremendous financial crisis.

One day early in July while I was home alone I began to cry out to God, asking Him why my personal needs were not being supplied. Although I knew the principles of faith and had witnessed to many thousands I had suffered serious financial reverses and had only enough money to cover my expenses for the rest of July. Looking ahead to August, I did not have the means to provide for my daily living expenses, much less to pay my house payment and utility bills. The needs were being met in the ministry to cover Sharon's salary and the salaries of our part-time workers. But I was taking none of this money to live on personally.

That morning a feeling of despair swept over me (which of course I never should have allowed in the first place — but remember, I am growing in the Lord, as you are). I fell on the floor crying and said, "Oh, God, have you brought me this far to abandon me? I've taught people that your Word is true. But now I can't pay my own bills. Am I going to have to give up the ministry and sell real estate?" The thought was unbearable, for I loved

How You Can Have Joy

working for the Lord. Yet it seemed I could no longer afford to continue in His service.

Later that day a letter came in the mail from a young woman whom I had met only once. It contained a prophecy which she said the Lord had impressed her to send to me immediately. The message of the prophecy was that God would provide for me, that He could make a way where there was no way, and that I should trust Him completely. If ever I needed to hear from God, it was on that day. I keep the letter even now and read it occasionally to remind me of God's faithfulness.

A week later a woman whom I knew only casually — she knew nothing about my personal life and very little about my ministry — called my mother and said, "Ruthe, I feel the Lord directing me to do something to help Vicki's ministry financially." Mother was excited and called me in Humble, Texas, where I was ministering, to give me the good news. I was elated. At this time there were numerous financial obligations in connection with our television show, "It's a New Day," and I thought she probably wanted to help with this.

This woman made an appointment with me to discuss my projects, and we met

The Joy of Receiving

around Mother's dining room table, which at that time was my office. The woman questioned me at length about what I felt the Lord leading me to do. Then quite unexpectedly she asked, "Do you need $6,000?"

I was momentarily taken aback. I hadn't expected such a straightforward question. Naturally, I could have used $6,000 in any number of places, as it was about $6,000 more than I had. But I could have used $50,000 with equal ease, for television is a very costly medium. I could not conscientiously tell her that there was a specific purpose for which I needed this exact sum. The only truthful answer I could give her was, "No, I don't need the specific amount of $6,000."

"Are you sure?" she asked. "God always deals with me in specific sums of money, and when He tells me a definite amount, there is always a definite need for this amount."

Again I assured her that I had no certain project which required exactly $6,000.

After some time she looked directly at me with her soft hazel eyes and said, "Vicki, what about you personally? What are you living on?"

Embarrassed, I stared down at my hands which were clasped on the table and studied them for some time. Finally, I stammered,

"Nothing in particular." (You see, I hadn't yet learned the art of being a gracious receiver.)

Then this godly woman, my mother and I sat and wept together quietly for several minutes, for Mother, who worked with me, knew of the financial pressures and of my great test of faith. God wanted to bless me. The $6,000 was intended for personal provision. It was an answer to the prayers of others, of which I knew nothing at that time. When I learned how faithfully and how exactly the Lord had answered those prayers my heart overflowed with joy, not only because of God's faithfulness, but because God had taught me an invaluable lesson in how to be a gracious and joyful receiver as well as a joyful giver, for it takes an abundant grace and humility to receive with thanksgiving and joy.

When you have experienced the heartwarming joy of receiving, you want to share this same joy with others. Therefore, you are eager to give in order that someone else can be as joyful in receiving as you were. While it is true that if you give you will receive it also follows that as you receive, it causes you to want to give.

Another unforgettable lesson the Lord taught me was in knowing how to be led by

The Joy of Receiving

the Holy Spirit in giving. At the same time He showed me the importance of receiving in a manner that will bless the giver as well as glorify the Lord.

One afternoon as I was driving home I began to think about a very close friend of mine. Suddenly I felt drawn to her. Rev. John Osteen calls this "the divine flow of love." When this happens you can be sure the person to whom you feel drawn has a need. Often the Lord is leading you to pray for that individual for a particular need, although this is not always the case.

In this instance I felt the urge to go to a grocery store and buy a ham for this woman. So strange and unusual was this impression that I wondered if I might not be going off the deep end. My friend lived in a lovely home with her husband and six children. Her husband had an excellent job. She certainly couldn't have a real need.

However, I couldn't shake this feeling, so I decided to put it to the test. I would see if I really did know the leading of the Holy Spirit.

Timidly I rang her doorbell, hoping — like the salesman who shouldn't be a salesman at all — that she wouldn't be home. For awhile it seemed she wasn't. Finally she answered

How You Can Have Joy

the door, surprised to see me for I had never before dropped in unannounced. Her look of surprise rapidly changed to one of bewilderment as I mumbled something about feeling led to bring this to her, and thrust a brown paper sack with a ham in it toward her.

She stumbled through a weak "thank you," and I turned to walk away, all the while thinking what a dunce I had been. Anyone could see she was anything but overwhelmed by my gift. Obviously she wasn't in dire need.

About halfway to my car I heard her call, "Wait!"

I walked back to the house and listened as she told me, somewhat reluctantly, how earlier that day she had discovered that she had no meat for dinner and that she was also without money in her household account. She had prayed, "Lord, if you want my family to have meat tonight, You will just have to send it." Although they could have easily survived without meat that night, the Lord heard her request and was pleased to answer. This ham had been God's way of showing her that He loved her family and was concerned about her needs, and that He wanted her to trust Him for everything.

Hearing this story gave me a greater boldness in trusting the leading of the Holy

How You Can Have Joy

Spirit in my own life. It also demonstrated the importance of showing appreciation and telling the person that his gift has come as an answer to prayer. For had my friend not shared this with me, I might not have realized that I really had heard the voice of the Holy Spirit. Because of her gratefulness in spite of a human reluctance to admit a need, this experience became a milestone for me in giving as well as in receiving, and was one I could look back upon when I was the one receiving instead of the one giving.

There are two extremes in the area of receiving, both of which, if we are not careful to avoid, will stunt our Christian growth and rob us of the joy which God intends should be ours. In the first extreme we see the individual who consciously or unconsciously becomes a professional "receiver," making his needs obvious so people will give to him. He is an opportunist who cultivates friendships advantageous to him, and uses people only as long as they can be of some benefit to him. Such is hardly a noble motive for receiving.

The other extreme involves the individual who has come to know the Lord and the power of His Word, and he knows that if he acts upon certain principles God will honor His Word and will abundantly supply every

How You Can Have Joy

need. This is good. However, although he may not be like the opportunist who says, "Please give me . . ." neither does he say "Thank you." Instead, he assumes the attitude: "God is my Source. Through Him all my needs are supplied; therefore, if I give thanks to man, I am not giving God the glory."

The statement, "God is my Source," is one that has been a motivating force in my life since I have been in the ministry. Time and again the Lord has proved to me that He is my Source. But it has always been through other people!

To refuse to express gratitude on the grounds that to do so would be giving credit to man rather than to God reflects not only poor judgment but also poor manners. Many who have been used of God in giving of their means — often with great sacrifice — have been deeply wounded by such seeming ungratefulness.

Observe on the other hand the apostle Paul's response to the generosity of the Philippian believers. His letter to them is a classic example of graciousness, courtesy and old-fashioned mannerliness. He begins by saying:

The Joy of Receiving

"I thank my God in all my remembrance of you. In every prayer of mine I always make my entreaty and petition for you all with joy (delight). (I thank my God)for your fellowship — your sympathetic cooperation and contributions and partnership — in advancing the good news (the Gospel) from the first day (you heard it) until now" (Phil. 1:3-5, *Amplified Bible*).

After further encouraging and instructing his friends at Philippi, Paul said, "Practice what you have learned and received and heard and seen in me, and model your way of living on it, and the God of peace — of untroubled, undisturbed well-being — will be with you" (Phil 4:9, *Amplified Bible*). Certainly good manners are as relevant in the 20th century as they were when Paul told us to follow his example.

Paul then wrote a beautiful "thank-you note."

"I was made very happy in the Lord that now you have revived your interest in my welfare after so long a time; you were indeed thinking of me, but you had no opportunity to show it . . . But it was right and commendable and noble of you to contribute for my needs and to share my difficulties with me. And you Philippians yourselves well know

How You Can Have Joy

that in the early days of the Gospel ministry, when I left Macedonia, no church (assembly) entered into partnership with me and opened up (a debit and credit) account in giving and receiving except you only. For even in Thessalonica you sent (me contributions) for my needs, not only once but a second time. Not that I seek or am eager for (your) gift, but I do seek and am eager for the fruit which increases to your credit — the harvest of blessing that is accumulating to your account. But I have (your full payment) and more; I have everything I need and am amply supplied, now that I have received from Epaphroditus the gifts you sent me. (They are the) fragrant odor (of) an offering and sacrifice which God welcomes and in which He delights. And my God will liberally supply (fill to the full) your every need according to His riches in glory in Christ Jesus" (verses 14-19, *Amplified Bible*).

Paul was able to express his gratitude to the Philippians for their liberality on his behalf and still give God the glory. He was not fearful of showing respect to man, nor did his gratefulness to the Philippians detract from his praise to God.

Paul was a gentleman. Even in difficult circumstances he showed his appreciation to his co-laborers as well as to those who supported

The Joy of Receiving

him financially. He was never in bondage because of their giving. He was confident in God to supply his needs. Therefore, without hesitation he could pen the promise which many of us have often used: "My God shall supply all your need according to his riches in glory by Christ Jesus" (Phil. 4:19). The principle of receiving which this verse speaks of was established because the people had followed the principle of giving. And Paul told them that their offerings had accumulated to their heavenly account.

Here were a people who because of their generous spirit Paul could say that as he prayed for them he did so with all joy. A joyful relationship resulted because the givers learned how to give and the receiver was not afraid to graciously receive, giving thanks to both God and man.

8
The Joy of Larry Lea

Larry Lea, the pastor of Church on the Rock in Rockwall, Texas, is a radiant young man from whom the joy of the Lord constantly emanates, overflowing to those around him. This was not always so, for at one point in his life his depression was so intense that he had to be hospitalized for treatment in a mental institution.

I want to share with you his testimony of how God brought him from the depths of despair and depression to a pinnacle of joyous praise in Him.

Larry Lea's Testimony

The joy which is ever-present in my life today is not my joy, it is the joy of the Lord. For I was once one of the most dejected persons in the world. We read in I John 1:3,4: "That which we have seen and heard declare

How You Can Have Joy

we unto you, that ye also may have fellowship with us: and truly our fellowship is with the Father, and with his Son Jesus Christ. And these things write we unto you, that your joy may be full." The greatest miracle in my life is the manifestation of this joy of the Lord in my soul.

My early teens were happy years — I was never down or depressed then. I enjoyed popularity, honors, and all the pleasures that money could buy. If material possessions could bring happiness and fulfillment in life, then I had all the credentials for successful living. For I was truly a "silver-spoon kid."

My family was wealthy and showered upon me all the things anyone could ever want. We were part of the country-club set in my hometown of Kilgore, Texas, and at the age of 16 I was driving an Oldsmobile 98 convertible. I was well liked by my classmates and earned various honors in my high school. In the University Interscholastic League drama competition, I won district, regional, and finally competed in the statewide contest, winning fourth place. I was active in all sports, expecially excelling in golf, in which I made all-state golfer, qualifying for state junior tournaments. I looked forward to a career in professional golf, and was

The Joy of Larry Lea

competing against some top players who are now professional golfers.

Although my family was rich in material things there was a poverty of the spirit in our home for my father was an alcoholic. Thus our home life was very unstable.

While in high school I attended the First Baptist Church in Kilgore, but I didn't really know Jesus. I had a religion but not a relationship. Inwardly I was pulled apart by the hypocrisy of my life, professing one thing on Sunday yet living another during the week. I put on a good show outside, but I was ever so empty inside. I longed for something more.

During the summer of 1968 my life began to fall apart. An unsuccessful romance caused me great mental anguish. I had discovered that money didn't bring satisfaction. Recognition and acclaim weren't enough. Now I realized that the girl whom I loved didn't fulfill the deep needs of my heart. Even the limited fame resulting from my achievements on the golf course seemed shallow and empty.

I began to withdraw from my family and friends. I couldn't sleep and began to lose weight. I couldn't express my emotions, but kept everything bottled up inside me. I never

How You Can Have Joy

became violent, but went to the other extreme of passiveness, alienation and melancholy. I even considered suicide several times. However, I didn't really want to die, yet I didn't want to live either. I couldn't cope with the frustration I felt.

Finally my parents began to realize that I had more than just a trivial teenage problem. They contacted my uncle, who is a doctor in New Orleans, and described my condition to him. He recommended that I be placed in the Mother Francis Hospital, Psychiatric Center, in Tyler, Texas, which is really a sophisticated mental institution for people who can afford private care rather than being committed to the state mental hospital in Terrell, Texas.

In the Psychiatric Center I was given 16 tranquilizers a day in addition to sleeping pills at night to help me rest. Yet my condition rapidly deteriorated. I was not suffering from a nervous breakdown but rather from a mental breakdown. My thought processes were deranged. I was convinced that the man across the hall was my doctor. I thought the black maid was my mother. I attached a name to everything — inanimate objects as well as people. I was paranoid, mistrusting

The Joy of Larry Lea

everybody. In my warped thinking every incident took on a sinister significance.

I can remember one thing which, looking back on it, seems humorous yet pathetic. The brand of toilet tissue used in the hospital was "Betty Ann." In my troubled mind I thought that this name of "Betty Ann" had been placed there to taunt me, for this was the name of one of my best friends.

Once my attention was drawn to a crucifix hanging on the wall of the lunchroom in this Catholic hospital. Examining it more closely I saw some Latin letters beneath it, and in my confusion I thought they spelled the name "Henry." I irrationally thought this was in derision of Jesus, and tearing the crucifix from the wall, I cried out, "His name is not Henry! *His name is not Henry!* His name is Jesus." Angrily I threw the crucifix in the trash, causing no small furor in this hospital, as can well be imagined.

Although I didn't realize it at the time, there was much prayer being offered in my behalf. My mother, an earnest and sincere Christian, was faithfully upholding me to God. Also, several prayer groups in Kilgore had taken me on their hearts.

During the first part of my stay in the hospital several different doctors were

How You Can Have Joy

assigned to my case. But nothing they did seemed to help. I feel it is not a coincidence that the doctor under whose care I was ultimately placed had had a born-again experience during his college years, although he did not fully understand what had happened to him. (Since then the Lord has allowed me to share with him the reality of Christ.)

After nearly four weeks in the hospital, I had lost 50 pounds and was showing no signs of improvement. Therefore, it was decided that I should have shock treatments. Three days before my first appointment in the shock room was scheduled, however, Jesus administered His own thrilling "shock treatment."

I had become desperate and began crying out to the Lord. I knew my only hope was in Him, even though I had no real knowledge of the Scriptures. I didn't know what to pray or how to pray, but I got down on my face in humility before the Lord and said the name of Jesus over and over again. "Jesus, Jesus, sweet Jesus," I repeated.

After calling on the name of Jesus in this manner, the Lord spoke to me — whether through an inner voice or an audible voice, I cannot be sure — and said, "You are going

The Joy of Larry Lea

to be a youth minister." At that time I didn't know what a "youth minister" was — I had never even heard the term. I only knew that God had spoken to me.

From that moment on there was a definite improvement in my condition. The sun was beginning to shine for me once again because God's Son had come into my life. Noticing the change, the doctor gradually reduced the heavy medication, cancelled the scheduled shock treatments, and two weeks after the Lord had spoken to me I was released from the hospital and went home.

As I mentioned earlier, I was privileged in that the doctor assigned to my case believed in God and therefore attributed my cure to the power of God. In fact, he has since written a report on my case stating that nothing he did brought about my cure, but that it was a miracle of God. What psychoanalysis and medication could not accomplish, God achieved through His miracle-working power.

My life took a different turn from then on and instead of being sad and depressed, I had God's wonderful joy.

On August 30, 1968, I was released from the hospital, and on September 1 I returned to high school to start my senior year. Of

How You Can Have Joy

course, the news of my confinement in a mental institution had drifted to my fellow students. So when I returned to school enthusiastic for the Lord and bubbling over with His joy, they thought I was still crazy. Now that I was turned on to the Lord instead of the devil, they couldn't understand it. However, by graduation time in the spring of 1969 I had won their respect and admiration to the extent that I was voted "the most talented student" in my high school.

After attending Kilgore Junior College for a year, I came to Dallas to attend Dallas Baptist College. I was able to receive my degree in only three years, graduating in 1972, which in itself was somewhat of a miracle. For before Christ came into my life I had been a rather poor student; now I was on the Dean's list every semester. My mental ability increased tenfold, and I could reason and concentrate as I had never been able to do before. While I had been in the depths of depression I didn't even know my own name; now I was studying Greek.

I didn't know anything about the Holy Spirit at that time; I just knew I had met the Lord and He was real and I wanted more of Him.

The Joy of Larry Lea

While studying at Dallas Baptist College I worked in several Baptist churches in the area. During this period I met the Reverend A. T. Ilseng, pastor of the New Testament Baptist Church, and under his ministry I received the baptism of the Holy Spirit in July, 1971. Then in April, 1972, the Reverend Howard Conatser asked me to be the youth minister at Beverly Hills Baptist Church in Dallas. I knew this was the fulfillment of God's promise to me — "You are going to be a youth minister." I accepted his invitation, and there the Lord richly blessed my labors for Him.

The Lord has given me a wonderful wife and three fine children. My entire family is now saved, and my father who had been a victim of alcoholism for twenty years was instantly delivered and is now an ordained Baptist deacon.

My ministry frequently leads me to help the mentally ill, the confused, those who have problems in this area, for it is an area of compassion for me. I can identify with their feelings, their longings, their needs. And I have the answer to give them: the Lord Jesus Christ. I tell them that fellowship with Jesus will bring about this same joy in their life that it has in mine.

How You Can Have Joy

This joy in my heart came about when God made contact with me one day, and I haven't gotten over it yet. It is a daily thing, a reestablishing of my commitment to Him, a fellowship which creates joy. If people are not experiencing joy, they are not experiencing Jesus.

Circumstances do not affect our joy. In fact, they have nothing whatsoever to do with it. Many people think that if all is going well, if conditions are just right, they can be happy, they will have joy. Yet Paul and Silas had such joy that even though they were in prison, they could sing praises to God while their backs were stinging from beatings.

In Galatians 5:22 we read that joy is one of the fruits of the Spirit. The joy I have is the joy of the Lord. If it is not His joy, I don't want it. As long as an individual stays in fellowship with Jesus, the result of this intimate relationship will be joy.

9
A Legacy of Joy

I had just finished taping my program, "Vicki," at Channel 40 in Los Angeles when Jan Crouch rushed in breathless, saying that it was time for her to do her evening program of sharing with the Trinity Broadcasting Network partners. This program is informal and keeps its viewers in touch with the television ministry and what is taking place in the lives being reached by it.

I scrambled off the set, and just as I was leaving Jan grabbed me and said, "Come and do this show with me." We sat in the midst of beautiful flowers and a fountain, and as the program progressed we found ourselves discussing her father, Edgar Bethany, who had recently gone to be with the Lord. He was a man well known in his denomination and greatly loved. Before I realized it, I was interviewing Jan on her own program, and a beautiful story unfolded. As I listened to Jan, I thought: What a wonderful experience to be able to share with others, for ultimately we will all lose a loved one, if we have not already done so. Jan's father left the earth in a sweet, victorious manner, beautifully illustrating what death can be for the Christian.

Jan is the wife of Paul Crouch, founder of Trinity Broadcasting Network in Los Angeles. Here in her own words is the touching story of her father's triumphant homegoing.

Jan Crouch's Testimony

Edgar Bethany was my best friend, my prayer partner, my pal and my Dad. Everywhere I went throughout the United States I could feel the love of total strangers flowing toward me when I would tell them, "I am Edgar Bethany's baby girl," because sometime in their lives they had been touched by this wonderful man.

Edgar Bethany was love — he loved Jesus with all his heart, soul and being. He lived Jesus — every day of his life. Now he has gone to be with Jesus where I know he is perfectly whole and happy.

A Legacy of Joy

I had never been able to let myself think of life on this earth without my Dad. But on October 16, 1975, he died. His prayers have ceased. His voice on the phone saying, "Baby, it's Daddy, and I've been praying for you today" is stilled. I can no longer look into his face and say, "Daddy, I love you."

But we are not sad. In fact, we have a joy we never had before. We have a joy which only Jesus can give, because we know where our Daddy is.

He taught me about heaven before he taught me the ABC's. He drew pictures of heaven on the easel of my mind before I was old enough to go to school. He spoke of the day when he would sit down with the apostle Paul. Now he can talk with the authors of the New Testament. Most important of all, he can put his arms around the One he loved and served for 55 years, his Saviour, his King, his Jesus.

My Dad was only five-feet eight-inches tall, but I never knew a man who stood taller. He never had much money, but he was meticulous in his appearance, always clean and neat, looking the very best he could. For he was a minister of the gospel of Jesus Christ, a privilege and responsibility he never took lightly.

How You Can Have Joy

Prior to October, 1975, I had never known my father to be ill. Since God had miraculously healed him of diabetes and heart trouble 38 years before, he had never had a sick day. But in the stillness of the night, October 2, 1975, I received the emergency message: "Your father has had a massive heart attack and is in intensive care in the hospital in Springfield, Missouri."

Suddenly I felt numb. My first reaction was that there had been a mistake. Daddy couldn't be seriously ill. He'll be all right. Then the reality hit me that he might not live — Daddy might die. My heart almost stopped beating. I've got to see my Daddy, I thought. "Oh, Jesus, please, I have to be with him. I have to touch him and talk to him. We have to pray together. I have to tell him that I love him. Please don't let my Daddy die."

During the flight from Los Angeles to Springfield, I could do nothing but cry and pray. I felt frightened and alone, afraid of the news that might greet me when I landed in Springfield. Suddenly God did a beautiful thing in my life. He had heard the heart-cry of a girl calling out to God for a miracle for her father. There in the plane God enveloped me in a bubble of love, a bubble of joy, a bubble of peace — a tingling, breathtaking

A Legacy of Joy

experience I had never had before. It was as if I were encased in a giant clear balloon. All I could do was to speak to my Heavenly Father in my heavenly language. So wonderful was this experience that I wanted to stay there forever. I felt as if I could have floated on up to heaven.

Then over the loudspeaker came the words, "We are arriving in Springfield. Please fasten your seat belts." I knew that in the hours to come I was to draw on my years of knowing and loving Jesus as I had never been called upon to do before. I was holding onto His promises as never before.

I was reluctant to look out the plane's window, afraid of what I might see on the face of my brother-in-law who was coming to meet me. Then slowly I turned to the window and saw him coming toward the plane. He was smiling. "Oh, thank you, Jesus!" I prayed. Quickly I gathered my things and pushed through the crowd to my brother-in-law. "Phil, how is Daddy?"

"Jan, he's alive. But let the doctor tell you."

When I arrived at the hospital the doctor said, "During the night your father's heart stopped. I happened to be in the hospital at the time and rushed in to resuscitate him. But I realized it was too late; there was nothing

How You Can Have Joy

we could do. Then for no apparent reason, his heart began to beat again. Your father is alive and wants to see you." All of this was happening, I realized, while Jesus was holding me in that beautiful bubble, and I was pleading with Him for Dad's life.

I walked into Dad's hospital room, and his eyes sparkled as he saw me running toward his bed. His arms stretched out toward me and we hugged and cried together. Then he told me of his experience the night before. "I felt my spirit leave my body last night. I was not one bit afraid. There was no fear. I knew I was going to be with Jesus, and it was wonderful. Then suddenly my spirit turned and re-entered my body. I don't know why my spirit returned, but it did."

With tears running down my cheeks, I whispered the most loving prayer I've ever whispered in my life. "Oh, thank you, Jesus. *I know why*, and I love you."

During the next few days Dad and I reminisced about all the lovely things we could recall. We talked about the miracles God had performed during his ministry, miracles of healing, miracles of lives that were changed and homes that were mended. And we talked about the miracle of Trinity Broadcasting Network. For Daddy loved TBN and

A Legacy of Joy

believed that television was the last great tool that Jesus had for winning the lost in these last days.

On Wednesday night, October 8, the night before I was to return home and to the ministry of PTL ("Praise the Lord," a TBN talk show), I lay awake in my darkened room, crying out to God for some answers. "God, please help me to understand what is happening. I don't understand why your choice servant is lying in the hospital, helpless. Why, God?"

The scripture flashed through my mind: "I have fought a good fight, I have finished my course, I have kept the faith . . ."

"Oh, no, God. Surely you are not through with Daddy. Surely he has not finished his course here. I need him. TBN needs him." But the rest of that scripture burned in my heart: ". . . Henceforth there is laid up for me a crown of righteousness . . ."(II Tim. 4:7,8).

As I talked that night with Jesus and He with me, I felt that same joy unspeakable, that same love of God encompassing me and holding me in a bubble of love. God held me that night, for He knew I would need His help. Three times in the night I felt this bubble of love encompass me, and three times

How You Can Have Joy

I was awakened speaking in my heavenly language.

At ten o'clock the next morning I went into Daddy's room. I leaned close to him and said, "Daddy, I'm going home today. I'll be on PTL. What do you want me to tell all those wonderful people who have been praying for you? When will you be back with them?"

His eyes filled with tears and he turned away. Slowly he turned his face toward mine, this time with a glow and a smile that I will remember until the day I see him again. He reached out his hands toward me and pulled me close. He said, "Just tell them to . . . keep praising the Lord."

I believe he knew he would not be back on PTL — ever. I believe that while God was holding me in His arms of love the night before, He was telling Daddy, "Edgar, you have fought a good fight. You have finished your course. You have kept the faith. Henceforth, there is laid up for you a crown of righteousness . . ." Daddy knew his life was over. His Father had told him.

Daddy kissed me and said, "Baby, I love you and you must *keep praising the Lord.*" With those words, I kissed my Daddy goodbye for the last time and returned to Los Angeles.

A Legacy of Joy

Had not the Lord been very near to me during the next few days, I could never have made it. For I longed to be with my father in that hospital room in Springfield. Each time the phone rang I froze, afraid of the news it might bring.

On Thursday night, October 16, Paul and I were hosts to Audrey Meier and Jim Spillman who were our special guests on PTL. We were sharing and singing and "praising the Lord," live on PTL when the phone captain tapped me on the shoulder. "Jan, there's an emergency call for you from Springfield."

"Oh, God, help me," my heart cried.

Picking up the phone, I heard my brother-in-law John say, "Jan, Papa went home to be with Jesus at 11:45 tonight."

The phone dropped into my lap and I began to sob. The news quickly traveled to my husband Paul who was before the live television cameras. As we had done many times before sharing with our TBN family everything, good and bad, that had happened in our lives, I knew I wanted to share this moment, too, with the people we loved so deeply. So I went back onto the PTL set, and clinging to Paul's strong arm with all my

How You Can Have Joy

might, together we shared the sad yet triumphant news of dad's homegoing.

As we drove home from the studio that night we felt an "arm of love" surrounding us, uplifting our spirits in a way I didn't know was possible. We knew the Lord's timing had been perfect in allowing this, the hardest moment of our lives, to happen while we were on live television in order that our TBN partners could uphold us with their love and prayers. That's what the arm of love was — the prayers of God's people.

Later I learned of the events of Daddy's last day on earth. He awoke quite early on the morning of October 16. My sister Dotty, her husband John, and Mother were with him. Because he was growing weaker the doctors had allowed them to be with him early that day. Daddy awoke with a greater calmness, joy and peace than he had had during the last few days. As he stirred he was smiling and motioned to Dotty to come close to his bed. She saw a joy on his face that was unmistakably Jesus. Daddy had talked to his Father that night, and he knew he was going home that day.

At fifteen minutes before midnight that night, Daddy closed his eyes and slipped into the arms of Jesus. He passed from this life

A Legacy of Joy

into heaven speaking to the One who was welcoming him home. He was talking to his Father in the language that only those two could understand. And the best part of it is that Satan couldn't understand one word of it.

As Mom, Dotty and John looked upon Daddy's still form, they did not see someone who was old, sick or sad. He seemed young, his face was full, his eyes were closed and he looked as if he were asleep. His lips formed a beautiful heavenly smile. He was happy, he was young, he was perfectly well and whole.

So how can I be sad? Oh, yes, I miss him and still want to see him. I still want to talk to him, pray with him. But I can't — because my Daddy is *home*. He's in heaven with Jesus. He's walking those golden streets where he is absolutely happy.

10
Sowing in Tears
. . . Reaping in Joy

In the fall of 1974 I found myself with a heavier schedule than I had ever had in my life. In addition to acting as hostess of the CBN television program, "It's a New Day," I was serving as producer as well. I had to help oversee the building and furnishing of the set, making sure it was finished on time. I was involved in wardrobe selection. I had to see that the sound tracks were recorded for a full season, which required a trip to Atlanta, Georgia. There were formats to prepare, and information to be developed on each guest to insure an interesting interview, plus a myriad of other details that go into producing a daily TV show. It seemed there weren't enough hours in a day, for in addition to the

How You Can Have Joy

television program, I was also engaged in a full-time ministry. At the same time I was in the midst of locating new office facilities for our staff and getting settled and organized in them.

Rather than doing "It's a New Day" live every day, we videotaped it in advance, recording several shows at a time. The days surrounding recording sessions were always extremely hectic and rushed. During this period of time my step-father became very seriously ill, suffering a series of strokes and very nearly dying. As we battled the illness that attacked him, it surely seemed as though all the powers of Satan were aligned against us, but God was preparing to give him a powerful testimony of healing, and He was preparing as well to teach me a lesson I would never forget — that the joy of my God is indeed my strength, spiritual as well as physical.

Here, in his own words, is my step-father's testimony to God's healing power:

Doyne E. Lamb's Testimony

On a Saturday afternoon in August of 1974, my wife Ruthe and I went with Vicki to look for new office space. At that time the

Sowing in Tears . . . Reaping in Joy

office was in our home, and the space was not adequate to accommodate the needs of Vicki's growing ministry. After looking over several facilities, we stopped to look at one more site. I hadn't mentioned it to anyone, but I had not felt up to par that day, so I waited in the car while Ruthe and Vicki went into the building. When they returned to the car they were aware that something was wrong with me, for although we were in a familiar part of the city I couldn't remember where I was. Vicki became alarmed. She had never been around anyone who had had a stroke, and so she didn't realize that this was what had happened to me.

They didn't wait until we got home to start praying for me, but immediately began to call upon God in my behalf as we drove along in the car. During the next few days prayers ascended to God constantly for my healing. Ruthe and Vicki as well as Vicki's co-workers, Sharon Bell-Stromley and Jeanne Kornhaber, took turns reading the Word of God aloud to me. They surrounded me with the Word of God, with faith-inspiring teaching on tapes, and with prayer for my healing. In such an atmosphere of faith, love and compassion, as I heard the Word of God repeated over and

How You Can Have Joy

over in my consciousness, I soon began to improve and was able to return to my work.

By mid-October we had obtained office space on the Christ for the Nations campus in Dallas, and were getting settled in the new offices when again we were to feel the blows of Satan. One morning I awoke in extreme pain in my lower back as well as in my left arm and leg. Ruthe went to Vicki's office and said to her, "We've got to pray for your father! Can you come over to the house right now?" Vicki immediately stopped what she was doing and came to my bedside where she and her mother began to intercede for me.

The next day, when the pain had not eased, I was taken to the hospital where a series of tests were run to determine its cause. I was placed in traction and given strong pain-killers. They tried diathermy and various types of therapy, all with no success. Then they ran a brain scan, milogram, and finally a neurosurgeon was called in. Several days passed before it was learned that I had suffered a stroke. I had lost my memory — I didn't know where I was or what was happening to me. I had also lost the use of my left leg.

Finally the doctor told my wife that there was nothing more they could do to help me,

Sowing in Tears . . . Reaping in Joy

so he released me and sent me home. My speech was slurred, my mind was vague, and I couldn't walk.

Three days after returning home from the hospital, as I awoke on that rainy, gloomy morning of November 6, 1974, I little realized what God had in store for me that day. I had been through so much that I sensed my suffering was to come to an end that day — the Lord was going to take me home to be with Him. Ruthe sensed this too.

Ruthe didn't want to call the doctor as she knew he could put me back in the hospital. In her spirit she just released me to God, believing that if it was God's time, she was ready to let me go. She felt no panic or fear, only the comforting presence of the Holy Spirit. She had a feeling of peace in spite of the fact that she knew I was dying.

We were all alone that day except for the nurse who came in twice to check my blood pressure. Although she didn't want to say anything to alarm Ruthe, she was quite concerned and felt that death was imminent. Vicki was away, ministering in Birmingham, Alabama, at the time.

Neither Ruthe nor I ate a bite of food all day. It seemed as if we were in another world apart from everyone else. We both felt as if

How You Can Have Joy

we were standing on tiptoe on the threshold of heaven. There was an atmosphere of absolute peace in our home as together we worshipped and praised the Lord and awaited His will. There was no apprehension or fear of death, only a keen awareness of God's presence.

Several times during the day I sensed the most beautiful fragrance I had ever smelled in my life — like no earthly fragrance imaginable. I kept saying to my wife, "Do you smell that heavenly fragrance?" But she could not smell what I was smelling.

While lying very still on my back, I looked up and suddenly it was as if a rectangular shaft had opened up into eternity. I could see, through what seemed to be an endless distance, into the glory land. I knew I was witnessing a tremendous sight. Then I saw twelve pillars. And there is no describing the beauty beyond those columns. It was like nothing I had ever seen. Truly, "Eye hath not seen, nor ear heard, neither have entered into the heart of man, the things which God hath prepared for them that love him" (1 Cor. 2:9). Fading into the distance were colors of a brilliance and hue I had never seen before on earth. They were beautiful, soothing, restful colors. But more awesome than the beauty

Sowing in Tears . . . Reaping in Joy

of the colors, or the fragrance of the flowers, was the all-encompassing love of God which engulfed me. God gave me a glimpse into heaven and into the magnitude of His love for me. It was as if there was no one else on earth, and that God loved me, just me, enough to send His Son to die for me that I could be with Him in His beautiful heavenly home forever.

Late in the afternoon I asked my wife, "What time will Vicki be returning?" I knew her plane was due sometime that evening.

"She arrives at 7:55," Ruthe answered.

I wanted to wait until Vicki came home before I left this earth to be with Jesus. I didn't want her to return to find me gone. I wanted her beside me when I departed this life.

When Vicki arrived from Birmingham she was met and asked, "Do you feel like going by to see your father before going home? I am sorry to have to tell you that he is very low."

At this same moment — 7:55 p.m. — suddenly a great cloud descended over me and seemed to engulf me in it. The glory of God completely surrounded me and I was immersed in God's healing power. Immediately I got out of bed and started walking around. Although I had had no use

How You Can Have Joy

of my left leg whatsoever prior to this, I was able to walk on it normally that night.

Ruthe had momentarily stepped into the kitchen, and when she returned to find me up, walking around the room and praising God, she was almost beside herself with joy, knowing what a great miracle of God she was witnessing.

Shortly after that Vicki walked in to find me — not flat on my back dying, but up, walking around, singing the praises of an all-powerful God.

The next day Satan attacked again and tried to rob me of my healing. I knew I had been miraculously healed and would not accept this attempt of Satan to steal from me my God-given victory. Although on this day I smelled the repugnant odor of death all day rather than the heavenly fragrance I had experienced the day before, we continually rebuked death, and before midnight had won the complete victory over the devil.

Even though the healing of my paralysis was instantaneous, it was a month or so before my mind was restored to normal. Our office staff banded together daily for my total deliverance, for we knew it was God's perfect will that I be completely healed. And although the second stage of my healing was

Sowing in Tears . . . Reaping in Joy

a gradual process, it was nevertheless as great a miracle as the instantaneous healing.

Vicki continues . . .

By December, 1974, my step-father's health was very nearly back to normal. I was alone one Saturday morning, looking forward to a leisurely, relaxing morning when my solitude was interrupted by the shrill ringing of the telephone. I reached for the phone, feeling somewhat resentful of its invasion of my quiet morning. On the other end of the line was a very close friend who needed some information. After I spoke with her a few minutes, she began to question me about the difficulties my family had been through during the past few months, and I related to her all the details of his marvelous deliverance and healing.

When I had finished telling her how God had delivered us through the trial we had just faced, I began to experience such joy that I literally felt physical power coming into my body. When I hung up the telephone, I began to praise God aloud and shout for joy. "Then was our mouth filled with laughter, and our tongue with singing: then said they among the heathen, The Lord hath done great things for them. The Lord hath done great things for us; whereof we are glad. Turn again our captivity, O Lord, as the streams in the south.

How You Can Have Joy

They that sow in tears shall reap in joy." (Psalm 126:2-5)

As I walked through my house intermittently praising and shouting and laughing, a supernatural strength flowed into my body, and for four days I was so empowered with a divine energy that I almost wondered if I would ever slow down again. I was wearing out my entire office staff as they tried to keep up with me while I moved from one project to the next, fortified with divine strength.

Prior to this time of trial and testing, the words of Nehemiah 8:10 had come to my mind time and again: ". . . The joy of the Lord is your strength." I kept wondering what God was trying to teach me or reveal to me. This day I became aware of the fact that when joy is released, it is released as we praise God for the great and mighty deeds He has done.

In the original Hebrew the word "joy" means "rejoicing, gladness, make glad, being joined." Also in the original Hebrew the term "Lord" is "Jehovah, the self-existent, eternal one, to exist, to cause to come to pass, to breathe, to be." The word "strength" means a "fortified place, a force, a fortress, a rock, a stronghold."

Knowing this we see that the scripture, ". . . The joy of the Lord is your strength,"

Sowing in Tears . . . Reaping in Joy

could be interpreted: "The rejoicing, being joined to Jehovah, the self-existent one, is my fortified place, my fortress, my stronghold."

With this light on the subject, I understood. I had experienced the rejoicing of my God who became a fortress from all of the assault of the enemy, protecting me with His Spirit and His Word. He became my spiritual as well as physical strength in a way I had never known before.

That day I saw what God was trying to teach me, and it was the beginning of a new adventure in releasing the joy of the Lord.

11
Why Do We Lose Our Joy

One discovery I have made is that when I lose my joy, I automatically know something spiritual is lacking in my life. Somewhere I am missing the perfect will of the Father. Perhaps it is because I am not having the daily fellowship with the Father I need and am not fortifying myself with His Word.

Shortly before Jesus died on the cross He prayed a prayer, not only for those who were His followers on earth at that time, but also for all who would ever receive Him in their hearts and make Him Lord of their lives. A portion of this prayer to the Father says, "And now I am coming to you. I say these things while I am still in the world, so that my joy may be made full and complete and perfect in them — that they may experience my delight fulfilled in them, that my enjoyment may be perfected in their own souls, that they

How You Can Have Joy

may have my gladness within them filling their hearts" (John 17:13, *Amplified Bible*).

The joy Jesus is speaking of that will be perfected in us can only come as we walk in fellowship with Him. And fellowship with Him is always evidenced by His love. The badge of true discipleship is love — that love which the world cannot comprehend that flows from the lives of others. Many times non-Christians have told me they didn't understand the love they felt emanating from our office staff on their behalf. This is the love which results from abiding in Christ.

When we step outside of this close relationship with the Lord, however, this joy that Jesus is speaking of begins to evaporate. Suddenly everything is drab and dreary, and we wonder why.

John 15:7 says, "If ye abide in me, and my words abide in you, ye shall ask what ye will, and it shall be done unto you." Many times we are so busy asking "what we will" that we fail to read the rest of that chapter. As we read further, however, we get an insight into the results of abiding in Christ and gain a new perspective on joy.

Verses 9-11 say, "I have loved you just as the Father has loved me: abide in My love — continue in His love with me. If you keep My

Why Do We Lose Our Joy?

commandments — if you continue to obey My instructions — you will abide in My love and live on in it; just as I have obeyed My Father's commandments and live on in His love. I have told you these things that My joy and delight may be in you, and that your joy and gladness may be full measure and complete and overflowing" (*Amplified Bible*).

Often when praying for specific things we do not wait for God's perfect plan but grasp the counterfeit which may arrive before the real manifestation of that answer to prayer. I learned this when I was praying that the Lord would send the right person to help in my ministry. I described to the Lord the exact qualifications for this person. Within two months a man came into my life who seemingly met every requirement. For some reason, though, I felt uneasy about him. But because he apparently qualified in every area, I overrode what I later discovered was a check in my spirit by the Holy Spirit.

Over a period of a month I discussed with him how he would work with me and what areas he would develop. During our talks I felt a hesitancy in my spirit, for I saw that his outlook on certain matters differed from mine. But it seemed I had no other way to turn at the time, and surely this man had

How You Can Have Joy

been the one whom the Lord had sent in answer to my prayers. Had I only listened to what my own spirit was telling me when my joy was replaced by unrest, I would have known it was not of God.

The evening came when I was to finalize my business arrangement with him. By this time the gnawing within me had become so intense that I said, "Oh, God, please give me a scripture to tell me what you really are saying." Immediately I felt led to open my Bible to the 16th chapter of Matthew. My eyes fell on the 26th verse, "For what will it profit a man if he gains the whole world and forfeits his life — his blessed life in the kingdom of God? Or what would a man give as an exchange for his blessed life — in the kingdom of God?" (*Amplified Bible*).

This scripture packed a powerful punch, and I realized that I was selling out. For I had considered ignoring certain principles I had always adhered to in order to meet the increasing financial demands of the ministry. I realized then that I had been walking away from certain faith principles and was depending upon the arm of man. And God had said it would profit me nothing if I gained the whole world.

Why Do We Lose Our Joy?

Then my spirit began to sing a song I had never sung in public. In fact, many times I had not considered it enough of a faith song. But now the melody and some of the words came into my mind and I began to hum it. I said, "Lord, where are the words to that song?" Within a matter of minutes He directed me to a tattered piece of music that had been given to me by a member of my family many years before. I stood in the center of my bedroom with the song in my hands, and with tears running down my cheeks I sang:

> If I gained the world, but lost the Saviour,
> Were my life worth living for a day?
> Could my yearning heart find rest and comfort
> In the things that soon must pass away?
> If I gained the world, but lost the Saviour,
> Would my gain be worth the life-long strife?
> Are all earthly pleasures worth comparing
> For a moment with a Christ-filled life?
>
> Had I wealth and love in fullest measure,
> And a name revered both far and near,
> Yet no hope beyond, no harbor waiting,
> Where my storm-tossed vessel I could steer;

How You Can Have Joy

If I gained the world, but lost the Saviour,
Who endured the cross and died for me,
Could then all the world afford a refuge,
Whither, in my anguish, I might flee?

Oh, the joy of having all in Jesus!
What a balm the broken heart to heal!
Ne'er a sin so great, but He'll forgive it,
Nor a sorrow that He does not feel!
If I have but Jesus, only Jesus,
Nothing else in all the world beside;
Oh, then ev'rything is mine in Jesus;
For my needs and more He will provide.

That night I went to the restaurant to meet the man. I told him I was sorry I had inconvenienced him, but I knew it was not God's will for us to work together. So dramatic a moment was this in my life, and so great a release had come through this song and a new determination that I would serve God in total purity, that I began to sing it for him. It was all I could do to keep from walking from table to table singing to every person there the meaningful song, "If I Gained the World but Lost the Saviour."

When I awoke the next morning every bit of darkness and oppression had lifted from my spirit. For the first time in a month I felt

Why Do We Lose Our Joy?

like getting out of bed. I knew my direction and that God was truly my source. Throughout the day I continued to sing, "If I Gained the World but Lost the Saviour," and then I would begin to sing, "The Joy of the Lord Is My Strength." My joy had returned. I was again walking in perfect fellowship with the Father, and I was now back into a love relationship with Him — one I had walked away from because of the conflict of walking apart from the will of God.

Joy cannot operate outside of God's perfect will for your life. If you have lost your joy, check up on yourself. Have you been having daily fellowship with the Father? Have you been spending time in praise and worship? Are you in harmony with those around you? For strife with others short-circuits our joy.

You can walk in joy as you walk in Him. Let His words abide in you and you abide in Him. Then you can ask what you will and it shall be done. Love as He loved, then His joy will be complete in you and your joy will be perfect in Him.

12 Lesson Series

Dynamics For Your Spiritual Growth

... from
Vicki Jamison-Peterson and her husband, Carl R. Peterson, M.D.

These twelve dynamic cassette tapes will be sent one a month each month for the next 12 months. Each tape will be a new session for your personal spiritual development. Experience spiritual growth and mental illumination through this dynamic presentation which has been carefully and thoughtfully taught by Vicki Jamison-Peterson, and Dr. Carl Peterson. (Dr. Peterson is a psychiatrist at the City of Faith; he is also an associate professor of Psychiatry at Oral Roberts University School of Medicine.) You will understand where the practice of medicine (man's God-given ability to heal) and your spiritual beliefs can be united without confusion by learning how your body, mind and spirit interact with God's spirit. Through these sessions you will build a strong base into your life so your full potential spiritually, emotionally and physically can be developed.

Using as an example the life of Christ Jesus, Carl and Vicki show how you can develop strength of character by using His Wisdom as you understand how He became great in Wisdom.

Also, they examine the area of relationships giving you solutions to help you in life's personal challenges.

Topics presented:
1. Power of Faith
2. Power of Strength, Confidence & Peace
3. Power of Order & Discipline
4. Power of Love
5. Power of Wisdom & Judgment
6. Power of Understanding
7. Power of Creative Spiritual Vision
8. Power of Will, Decision & Action
9. Power of the Word
10. Power of Joy, Enthusiasm and Zeal
11. Power of Renunciation or Elimination
12. Power of Life or Healing Power

By becoming a $15.00 monthly partner for a year, you will receive:
- An audio cassette each month on the subjects listed above.
- An outline of each lesson.
- Questions for you to answer on each subject to help you learn — at your request.

Coupon on opposite page.

OTHER MATERIALS AVAILABLE BY VICKI JAMISON-PETERSON

Tape Series Titles	No. of Tapes in Series	Price

FAITH SERIES (2) $10.00
The weapon and confession of faith brings the operation of faith into the realm of your day-to-day living. How to develop your faith to start receiving answers you need from God.

FOUR GOSPELS (8) $30.00
Now, in the privacy of your own home, the Four Gospels come alive on cassette tape. You will thrill to the sound of Jesus' words as He preached to the multitudes, performed miracles, and taught His disciples. Beautiful instrumental background music and special effects on the words of Jesus.

WINNING WITH GOD (4) $20.00
To help you "forget the past", and "look forward to the goal in Christ Jesus", we offer these seven 30-minute teaching tapes on reaching your goals. Listen to a new lesson every day of the week — re-listen the next week and after a month you will be convinced that you can "Win With God".

HOW TO REACH FOR YOUR STAR (4) $20.00
God is bigger than your biggest dreams and Vicki shares God's principles for making your dreams come true. Teaching on a practical, understandable level that lets you know what to do when everything is going in reverse. This will put you on the road to God's highest and best for you. It is life changing!

Vicki,   **CLIP THIS COUPON — MAIL TODAY**

☐ Please enroll me as a seed-faith partner for $15.00 a month, or more.

☐ Send me a tape a month for a year and an outline of the subjects you and Dr. Peterson teach.

☐ Please include the list of questions and enroll me in the course. I desire to receive a special Achievement Certificate from you and Dr. Peterson.

Enclosed is my first monthly pledge in the amount of $_____.

SEND ORDER TO:

NAME _____ ADDRESS _____

CITY _____ STATE _____ ZIP_____

Mail to:
Vicki Jamison-Peterson
P.O. Box 700030
Tulsa, OK 74170

EACH MONTH CHARGE IT TO MY:	MasterCard	Visa
Card Exp. Date: Month		Year
CARD NUMBER: ☐☐☐☐☐☐☐☐☐☐☐☐☐☐		
Signature:		

DECIDE TO PROSPER (2) $10.00
Do you find it hard to believe that God has a super-abundance of all good things for you? Are you afraid to prosper? If you answered yes, you need this Bible-based, anointed teaching. Vicki's message can transform your life and teach you how to start enjoying divine prosperity — physically, financially, spiritually, and emotionally!

HOLY SPIRIT SERIES (3) $15.00
This series will help you begin to recognize the activity of the Holy Spirit in your personal life, and to learn to acknowledge Him as a person. You will learn to practice His presence and develop your prayer language.

THE WHOLE PERSON (4) $20.00
Taught by Vicki & Dr. Peterson
Learn how to better resolve conflicts and relationship problems within the area of family, friends and personal growth. These tapes will be "a lifeline" to build your faith and help you to understand the spiritual principles involved.

RELEASING GOD'S POWER (2) $10.00
You have within your spirit enough power to shake your entire city for Christ! The secret is in releasing it. God has so many wonderful things planned for your life . . . so many miracles He wants to perform through you. Learn to operate in His Kingdom at peak potential.

MIND OF CHRIST (2) $10.00
Learn the secret of thinking the thoughts of God. Discover how to think your way through the Bible to succeed in every part of your life — mentally, physically, spiritually, and financially. Hear practical instructions and examples of goal setting, imagery, creative habit development, and the Christ controlled mind.

Record & Tape Order Blank:

QTY.	TITLE	AMOUNT
____	_____	_____
____	_____	_____
____	_____	_____
____	_____	_____

Amount Enclosed _____

Send order to:

Name _____ Address _____

City _____ State _____ Zip _____

Make checks payable to: Vicki Jamison-Peterson
Please include full payment with order.
All prices include postage and handling.
(Bookstore discount available upon request.)

Mail to:
Vicki Jamison-Peterson
P.O. Box 700030
Tulsa, OK 74170

Recordings

Cassette — $8.00
LP   — 4.00

EL SHADDAI

EL SHADDAI
FLYING AWAY
SAY THE WORD
LET YOUR FAITH DO THE
  WALKIN'
HOW GREAT THOU ART
HOLY SACRIFICE

HOLY SPIRIT MEDLEY
  Holy Spirit, Thou Art
    Welcome in this Place
  Holy Spirit, Flow through me
COME LET US BOW DOWN
KNOWIN' HE CARES
SACRIFICE OF PRAISE

FORGETTING THOSE THINGS BEHIND

LORD, TAKE ME HIGHER IN YOU
BLESSED ASSURANCE
MEDLEY:
  All Hail The Power Of
    Jesus' Name
  Crown Him With
    Many Crowns
  Praise Him! Praise Him!
DOXOLOGY: PRAISE GOD,
  FROM WHOM ALL
  BLESSINGS FLOW

AMAZING GRACE
JESUS IS THE CORNERSTONE
GLORY TO HIS NAME
MEDLEY:
  O Come, Let Us Adore Him
  Joy To The World!
MEDLEY:
  Victory In Jesus
  Victory

RISE AND BE HEALED

RISE AND BE HEALED
WHO SHALL HIS GENERATION
  DECLARE
THEY OVERCAME HIM
MEDLEY:
  I Want To Be Like Jesus
  Jesus Never Forgets
SEED OF ABRAHAM

I BELIEVE IN GOD
BECAUSE HE TOUCHED ME
MEDLEY:
  Do You Love Me
  Love Would Not Let Him
    Forget
THE EASTER SONG
FAITH IS

Hearing from you blesses me...

Your faith is released when you write a letter. You have then turned your care over to God for the answer you need.

When I hear from you I will pray for your needs — we will rejoice as the Father sets miracles in motion for you.

Address your letter to:

Vicki Jamison-Peterson
P.O. Box 700030
Tulsa, OK 74170